SAP™ R/3
ABAP/4

Command Reference

SAP™ R/3 ABAP/4

Command Reference

Dennis Barrett

SAP™ R/3 ABAP/4 Command Reference

Copyright© 1997 by Que® Corporation.

Library of Congress Catalog No.: 97-68102

ISBN: 0-7897-1416-7

99 98 97   6 5 4 3 2 1

Interpretation of the printing code: the rightmost double-digit number is the year of the book's printing; the rightmost single-digit number, the number of the book's printing. For example, a printing code of 97-1 shows that the first printing of the book occurred in 1997.

All terms mentioned in this book that are known to be trademarks or service marks have been appropriately capitalized. Que cannot attest to the accuracy of this information. Use of a term in this book should not be regarded as affecting the validity of any trademark or service mark.

Screen reproductions in this book were created by using Collage Plus from Inner Media, Inc., Hollis, NH.

Contents at a Glance

Table of Contents

SAP R/3 ABAP/4 Command Reference

SAP R/3 ABAP/4 Command Reference

Contents

SAP R/3 ABAP/4 Command Reference

Contents

SAP R/3 ABAP/4 Command Reference

Contents

Credits

President
Roland Elgey

Senior Vice President/Publishing
Don Fowley

Publisher
Stacy Hiquet

Senior Title Manager
Bryan Gambrel

General Manager
Joe Muldoon

Director of Editorial Services
Carla Hall

Managing Editor
Caroline D. Roop

Director of Acquisitions
Cheryl Willoughby

Acquisitions Editor
Angela C. Kozlowski

Senior Editor
Mike La Bonne

Editor
Aaron Gordon

Coordinator Editorial Resources
Maureen McDaniel

Product Marketing Manager
Kourtnaye Sturgeon

Assistant Product Marketing Manager
Gretchen Schlesinger

Technical Editor
Brian Bokanyi, senior consultant, CAP Gemini

Software Specialist
Brandon K. Penticuff

Software Coordinator
Andrea Duvall

Acquisitions Coordinator
Carmen Krikorian

Software Relations Coordinator
Susan D. Gallagher

Editorial Assistants
Travis Bartlett
Jennifer L. Chisolm

Book Designer
Ruth Harvey

Cover Designer
Nathan Clement

Production Team
Marcia Deboy
Bryan Flores
Trey Frank
Julie Geeting
Nicole Ruessler
Donna Wright

Indexers
Ginny Bess
Tina Trettin

Composed in Frutiger and ITC Kabel by Que Corporation.

To my joyous wife Joya.

Thanks to Tipton Cole for every sort of assistance and permission to use York-Mills Notation, and to John Keating and Hart Graphics for their support and access to the Release 2.2 system.

About the Author

Dennis Barrett is the SAP project leader at Hart Graphics in Austin, Texas. He's been programming and developing database applications for over 12 years in several different programming languages. He received his certification as an ABAP programmer from the SAP Partners Academy over a year ago and has been writing ABAP/4 programs ever since. He's a graduate of the University of Texas in mathematics and physics, and has attended several courses provided by SAP in ABAP/4, Basis and Materials Management. Dennis is the co-author of "ABAP/4 Programming Guide," which is also published by Que Computer Books. He is the founding chairperson of the Small Businesses Interest Group of the Americas' SAP User Group (ASUG).

We'd Like to Hear from You!

As part of our continuing effort to produce books of the highest possible quality, Que would like to hear your comments. To stay competitive, we *really* want you to let us know what you like or dislike most about this book or other Que products.

Please send your comments, ideas, and suggestions for improvement to:

The Expert User Team

E-mail: **euteam@que.mcp.com**

Fax: (317) 581-4663

Our mailing address is:

Expert User Team
Que Corporation
201 West 103rd Street
Indianapolis, IN 46290-1097

You can also visit our Team's home page on the World Wide Web at:

http://www.mcp.com/que/developer_expert

Thank you in advance. Your comments will help us to continue publishing the best books available in today's market.

Thank You,

The Expert User Team

INTRODUCTION

This book is a reference guide to ABAP/4, the programming language for SAP R/3. This chapter outlines the structure of ABAP/4 Command Reference.

The SAP (we say S. A. P. not "sap") R/3 enterprise application uses the ABAP/4 programming language to construct many of its features, and developers may use ABAP/4 to prepare custom reports, import legacy data, design online transactions, and perform other programming tasks. Indeed, most of R/3 was written in ABAP/4. The name stands for "Advanced Business Application Programming, Fourth Generation."

This reference is intended to provide a concise, accurate, and accessible summary of the main elements of R/3 and ABAP/4 that a developer needs to do that work. Specifically, the reference lists the syntax of commands, most of their options ("additions" in SAP lingo), pointers to related commands, and some of the "magic words" found in the R/3 world.

This book is intended for the convenience of trained, experienced ABAP/4 programmers, and not as an introduction to ABAP/4 or as a teaching tool. However, it may be useful to students of ABAP/4 as a supplement to textbooks and other training materials.

Some of the commands have variants not described herein. In the spirit of a quick reference, I have covered the variants that appear to be in common use and left out the more obscure ones. See the Online Help for more variants to those commands. I haven't included commands shown in the Online Help as "for internal use only" or as obsolete.

There appear to be variants that SAP has not documented. Have a look at some native SAP programs, and you'll often find very interesting uses of commands that don't show up in the Online Help or the manuals. I've included very few of these, since they're likely to be unstable between releases, and labeled them as "undocumented."

Introduction

The ABAP/4 language grows and changes through the revisions. These descriptions apply to Releases 2.2 and 3.0, except commands and options marked [3.0], which apply only to Release 3.0.

This reference uses typefaces and symbols as follows:

- **keyword**—e.g., ABAP/4 command, event, option, etc.
- `sy-variable`—System variables
- itab—The literal name of an internal table
- f1, f2, f3—Literal field names and formal parameters
- a1, a2—Actual parameters
- dbtab—Literal names of database tables
- <value>—Either a literal number or string, or a variable
- arrayname—Literal name of a data structure
- [command option]—An option on the main command is enclosed in square braces; the braces are not typed in the program
- [command option...]—The option may be repeated some number of times; the braces are not typed in the program
- {alternate1 | alternate2}—Alternative options are shown separated by pipes (vertical lines) and enclosed in braces; the pipes and braces are not typed in the program

For example, the `assign` command and its options (additions) are as follows:

```
assign
{ [local copy of] {f1[+p1][(w1)] | (f2) }
| component f3 of structure array1}
to <fs> [type t1] [decimals d1]
```

The `assign` command is interpreted as follows:

`assign` must assign to `<fs>` either
```
f1 or
(f2) or
component f3 of structure array1.
```

If it was followed by f1, then it could actually assign the substring of f1 defined by its offset [+p1] or its width [(w1)].

If it was followed by either f1 or (f2) and the statement was in a subroutine, then it could assign a local copy of f1 or (f2) in the subroutine.

The command may assign a TYPE to the target.

The command may assign a DECIMALS value to any Type P target.

SAP R/3 provides a huge capability to interactive users who enter commands at the menus and screens. In order to have a convenient and concise way to record those commands, I have included the separately developed *York-Mills Notation* in Part XII with permission of the authors. That specification provides a way to publish the interactive command sequences shown in this reference.

Why Use ABAP/4?

People use ABAP/4 because it is the language provided with SAP R/3, and is the only way to develop custom reports, interfaces to other systems, and user transactions for R/3.

Integration with R/3

Everything in R/3 is in tables, including the source for ABAP/4 programs. That source can include code and several objects stored separately from the code: "text elements"—(labels, headings, and the like), graphical screens, and menus. The programming environment is quite visual, and difficult to imagine or simulate outside an R/3 system.

Rapid Development

Many programming projects are high level rather than low level. That means that they tend not to involve bit-level manipulations, direct operating system calls. Instead, they focus on reading from tables and files, reformatting the output, and writing it. With ABAP/4, the programmer does not need to get involved in the details of how file handles and buffers are manipulated, how memory is allocated, and so on. It's fairly easy to read even without knowing any ABAP/4, especially if you are familiar with languages like Basic or Pascal.

ABAP/4 feels clunky. It appears to have grown out of a blend of assembler, COBOL, RPG, and SQL. ABAP/4 commands can look and feel a bit different from each other, depending on their heritage, which leads to the great value of a reference work: it's tough to memorize this command set. The language is powerful for its purpose; you can rather quickly code, test, and deliver to the user a custom report.

Compiler and Interpreter

A program by itself can't achieve anything. To carry out its work, it needs to be fed to either a compiler or an interpreter. Both have their advantages:

- A compiler takes a program listing and generates an executable file. This executable file can then be executed as many times as necessary, copied to other computers, and so on without the need for the program source code. This helps to keep program details confidential.

- Because the compiler runs only once, it can afford to take its time generating executable code. As a result, compilers tend to perform elaborate optimization on the program code with the result that the executable code runs very efficiently.

- An interpreter examines a program listing line by line and carries out the tasks required by the code there and then. There is no need for a separate compilation stage; once the program has been written, it can be executed without delay. This makes for a rapid development cycle.

There are advantages and disadvantages to each approach. Compiled code takes longer to prepare, but then it runs fast and your source stays secret. Interpreted code gets up and running quickly but isn't as fast as interpreted code. You also need to distribute the program source code if you want to allow others to run your interpreted programs.

So which of these categories describes ABAP/4?

Well, ABAP/4 is a little special in this regard; it is a compiler that thinks it's an interpreter. ABAP/4 compiles program code into executable code before running it, so there is an optimization stage and the executable code runs quickly. However, it doesn't write this code to a separate executable file. Instead, it stores it in memory and then executes it.

This means that ABAP/4 combines the rapid development cycle of an interpreted language with the efficient execution of compiled code. The corresponding disadvantages are also there, though: The need to compile the program each time it runs means a slower startup than a purely compiled language and requires developers to distribute source code to users.

In practice, these disadvantages are not too limiting. The compilation phase is extremely fast, so you're unlikely to notice much of a lag between invoking an ABAP/4 program and the start of execution.

In summary, ABAP/4 is compiled "behind the scenes" for rapid execution, but you can treat it as if it is interpreted. This makes it easy for you to tweak your application; just edit the code and let the users run it. But is that good programming practice? Hey, that's one for the philosophers.

Flexibility

ABAP/4 was not designed in the abstract. It was written to develop the SAP enterprise application and it evolved to serve an ever widening set of business problems that SAP addresses.

The Structure of This Book

This book falls into two sections. The first includes the introduction, an overview, and Part I, which is an alphabetical reference to the keywords in the ABAP/4 language. The second includes Parts II through XII, which show detailed information in tables and examples.

- The overview briefly introduces the basic concepts of programming in ABAP/4.

- The alphabetical reference describes all the ABAP/4 variables, operators, and functions in one long section.

- The rest of the parts list fields, tables, transactions, and utilities, and show examples of some of the more complex things you might want to do in ABAP/4.

Since all the keywords are covered in the alphabetical reference section, an index, and glossary would be redundant, and are not included.

OVERVIEW

A BAP/4 Command Reference is designed as a reference guide for the ABAP/4 language, rather than an introductory text. However, there are some aspects of the language better summarized in a short paragraph as opposed to a table in a reference section. Therefore, this chapter puts the reference material in context, giving an overview of the ABAP/4 language.

Running ABAP/4

The simplest way to run an ABAP/4 from inside SAP R/3 is to execute the transaction SA38. To do this, follow these steps:

1. Type /NSA38 in the command field.
2. Press Enter.
3. Type the name of the ABAP/4 program in the resulting blank field.
4. Press Enter.

There is no way to run an ABAP/4 program outside of an SAP system.

An ABAP/4 Script

An ABAP/4 program is stored in an SAP table as a series of ABAP/4 commands; it is executed from a memory image of those commands. Commands are written in what looks like an amalgam of assembler, COBOL, RPG, and SQL. In fact, that's pretty much what it is. The memory image can be uploaded from and downloaded to a normal ASCII text file for documentation or other purposes, but only the memory image can be executed.

An ABAP/4 Script

The easiest way to go into the ABAP/4 Editor to create or edit programs is by typing **/nSE38 <Enter>** in the command field.

ABAP/4 code can be quite free-flowing. The broad syntactic rules governing where a statement starts and ends are as follows:

- Leading white space is ignored. You can start an ABAP/4 statement anywhere you want: at the beginning of the line, indented for clarity (recommended), or even right-justified (definitely frowned on) if you like. Lines may be up to 72 characters long.
- Commands are terminated with a period.
- White space outside of string literals is irrelevant; one space is as good as a hundred. That means you can split most statements over several lines for clarity, and you can place several short commands on the same line.
- Literal strings are delimited by single-quotes (').
- Anything on a line after a double-quote (") is ignored, and any line beginning with an asterisk (*) is ignored. Use this to pepper your code with useful comments. The next line break ends the comment.
- ABAP statements take the following form:

```
Keyword    parameters & data objects    period(.).
```

Many statements may follow the keyword with a colon (:) and accept comma-separated multiple predicates; each element (keyword, parameter, grouping parentheses) must be separated by one or more spaces or a line break. Case is not distinguished by the processor, except for string comparisons; you are free to use case to enhance readability.

Here's an ABAP/4 statement inspired by Kurt Vonnegut (An Indiana author whose works show compassion and humor in the midst of the violence and alienation of modern life. His novels include *Cat's Cradle* and *Slaughterhouse Five*):

```
WRITE 'My name is Yon Yonson'.
```

No prizes for guessing what happens when ABAP/4 runs this code; it prints

```
My name is Yon Yonson
```

Printing more text is a matter of either stringing together statements or giving multiple arguments to the print function, such as:

```
WRITE      'My name is Yon Yonson,'.
WRITE: /  'I live in Wisconsin,',
       /  'I work in a lumbermill there.'.
```

If the / doesn't look familiar, don't worry; it simply means that ABAP/4 should print a new line character; in other words, ABAP/4 should go to the start of the next line. In ABAP/4 you generally place it before the string instead of after it. The first slash needn't be comma-separated, but all the rest of them must be.

Notice that I strung together the second and third print lines in the same WRITE statement by using commas, that second command spans two lines, and the extra spaces on the third line don't affect the result:

```
My name is Yon Yonson,
I live in Wisconsin,
I work in a lumbermill there.
```

That's not at all typical of an ABAP/4 program though; it's just a linear sequence of commands with no structural complexity. The "Branch Control" section later in this overview introduces some of the constructs that make ABAP/4 what it is. For now, we'll stick to simple examples like the preceding for the sake of clarity.

Data Types

ABAP/4 has several native data types and has the means for you to define your own complex types from the native ones. Those complex types can include arrays whose elements have differing types; indeed any one such element can be a table with any number of records. See "Type" in the alphabetical section for a description of each of the native types.

Variables

Variables or fields may be of any native or user-defined type. Variable names are limited to 30 characters and must include at least one nonnumber character; they may not include spaces, parentheses, plus, minus, or hyphen signs, commas, or periods. These names are case-insensitive.

Variables

ABAP/4 converts automatically between types wherever it makes sense. All of these conversions are handled implicitly, leaving the programmer free to concentrate on what needs to be done rather than the low-level details of how it is to be done.

We can use variables to develop the earlier example script by using some string variables:

```
DATA:
  who(10)  VALUE 'Yon Yonson',   "defaults to
character type
  where(9) VALUE 'Wisconsin',
  what(15) VALUE 'in a lumbermill'.


WRITE:
'My name is', who NO-GAP, ',',
    / 'I live in',  where NO-GAP, ',',
    / 'I work', what, 'there.'.
SKIP 1.
WRITE: / 'Signed:', 12 who, /12 where NO-GAP, '.'.
```

which yields:

```
My name is Yon Yonson,
I work in Wisconsin,
I work in a lumbermill there.

Signed:     Yon Yonson,
            Wisconsin.
```

I've declared several variables with the DATA statement, assigned their initial values with the VALUE options, and added some formatting. The WRITE command usually separates fields with one space, but I made the comma immediately follow "Yonson" by specifying the NO-GAP option, and I added a blank line before his signature with the SKIP 1 command.

Branch Control

The examples we've seen so far have been quite simple, with little or no logical structure beyond a linear sequence of steps. ABAP/4 has the following branch control mechanisms (see their descriptions in the alphabetical section for details):

- IF condition...ELSEIF condition2...ELSE...ENDIF
- DO [n TIMES]...ENDDO
- WHILE condition...ENDWHILE

For specific situations:

- LOOP...ENDLOOP

Conditional Expressions

You may use several forms of conditional (logical) expressions. See "Condition" and "Operators" in the alphabetical section for the details.

Subroutines

Subroutines in ABAP/4 are code blocks `labeled FORM formname...ENDFORM`. You can pass arguments to and from forms by value or by reference, and you can pass working tables to and from them. A form is called by the PERFORM formname command. Forms may call other forms and they may call themselves (recursion).

REFERENCE (ALPHABETICAL)

= (equals sign)

Compliance

| 2.2 | 3.0 |

Definition

"Equality" relational operator (same as EQ), and assignment operator; multiple assignments are supported and are processed from right to left.

Example

```
x = y = 3 .
WRITE: 'x =', x, ';   y =', y.
   → x = 3 ;   y = 3
```

Cross-reference

See also Operators, MOVE, WRITE TO

*tablename

Compliance

Definition

For any database table that you declare in a TABLES statement (such as kna1), you can also declare a work area with the same structure using its name preceded by an asterisk (*kna1).

Example

```
TABLES: kna1, *kna1.
```

Cross-reference

See also Work area

Work area

Compliance

Definition

A work area is a field array that matches the structure of a database or internal table. In most cases, you move data between the table and the work area and do most of your table-related work in the work area.

When you declare a database table in a TABLES statement, R/3 automatically defines a header-line work area with the same name as the table. At that time you can also declare an additional independent work area by including in the TABLES statement the tablename preceded by an asterisk.

When you declare an itab using BEGIN OF...INCLUDE STRUCTURE or LIKE...WITH HEADER LINE, R/3 automatically defines a header-line work area with the same name as the itab.

You can manually define a work area in a DATA statement using the INCLUDE STRUCTURE tablename or LIKE tablename constructions. Or you can (oh my!) manually define a work area in a DATA statement by explicitly calling out all the fields with their widths and types.

Example

```
*Illustrate identical results from different types
of work area
TABLES: kna1, *kna1.
DATA: BEGIN OF wkna1.
   INCLUDE STRUCTURE kna1.
DATA: END OF wkna1.
DATA: BEGIN OF ikna1 OCCURS 12.
   INCLUDE STRUCTURE kna1.
DATA: END OF ikna1.


*Demonstrate implicit header line of database table
WRITE 'kna1'.
SELECT * FROM kna1 WHERE kunnr LT '0000100012'.
   WRITE: / kna1-kunnr.
ENDSELECT.
BACK.


*Demonstrate "star" header line of database table
WRITE 15 '*kna1'.
SELECT * FROM kna1 INTO *kna1 WHERE kunnr LT
'0000100012'.
   WRITE: /15 *kna1-kunnr.
ENDSELECT.
BACK.


*Demonstrate explicitly defined header line
WRITE 30 'wkna1'.
SELECT * FROM kna1 INTO wkna1 WHERE kunnr LT
'0000100012'.
   WRITE: /30 wkna1-kunnr.
```

Work area

```
ENDSELECT.
BACK.

*Demonstrate itab header line
WRITE 45 'iknal'.
SELECT * FROM knal INTO TABLE iknal WHERE kunnr LT
'0000100012'.
LOOP AT iknal.
  WRITE: /45 iknal-kunnr.
ENDLOOP.
```

Cross-reference

See also Header line

ABS

Compliance

2.2 3.0

Syntax

```
ABS( x ).
```

Definition

Absolute value of any number x.

Cross-reference

See also Arithmetic functions

ACOS

Compliance

3.0

Syntax

`ACOS( y ).`

Definition

Arc-cosine of floating point number y, for y between -1 and +1, and `ACOS( y )` between 0 and Π.

Cross-reference

See also Arithmetic functions

ADD

Compliance

| 2.2 | 3.0 |

Syntax

`ADD a TO b.`

Definition

Equivalent to $b = b + a$. Non-numeric fields are converted; see Part VIII, "Type Conversions" for conversion information.

Cross-reference

See also `DIVIDE, MULTIPLY, SUBTRACT`

ADD-CORRESPONDING

Compliance

| 2.2 | 3.0 |

Add-Corresponding

Syntax

```
ADD-CORRESPONDING array1 TO array2.
```

Definition

If `array1` and `array2` are structured work areas such as header lines, then this command adds **like-named** fields in `array1` and `array2`. It's equivalent to:

```
ADD array1-key1 TO array2-key1.
ADD array1-key2 TO array2-key2.
...
```

Cross-reference

See also ADD, `DIVIDE-CORRESPONDING`, `MOVE-CORRESPONDING`, `MULTIPLY-CORRESPONDING`, `SUBTRACT-CORRESPONDING`

addition

Definition

An "addition" in SAP lingo is an optional parameter that expands the function of its base command.

Example

In the following description of `APPEND`, the six additions are:

- `wa TO itab1`,
- `INITIAL LINE TO itab1`,
- `LINES OF itab2 TO itab1`,
- `FROM ndx1`,
- `TO ndx2`, and
- `SORTED BY f1`.

In this reference manual, optional parameters are indicated by the square braces [ ] in the command description, and alternatives among

Function	Description	Compliance

those options are separated by the "pipe" or vertical bar (l). If one of several parameters **must** be used, the list of parameters is enclosed in curly braces ({ }), and the parameters in the list are separated by vertical bars. Don't type the braces or vertical bars in your programs.

APPEND

Compliance

| 2.2 | | 3.0 | for the main command

| 3.0 | for options marked with [3.0]

Syntax
APPEND

[wa

| INITIAL LINE [3.0]

| LINES OF itab2 [FROM ndx1] [TO ndx2]] [3.0]

itab1

[SORTED BY f1].

Definition

Appends a new record to the end of itab1 from its header line, from work area wa, or from an initial-value (that is, cleared) structure. Appends records from itab2 to the end of itab1, starting with the first record of itab2 or from record ndx1 if it is specified, and continuing to the last record, or record ndx2, if it is specified. There's no limit to the number of records itab1 may accept. Both wa and itab2 must have the same structure as itab1. SORTED BY f1 sorts itab1 on field f1 after the record is appended, then truncates the table to the number of records in the OCCURS declaration (This option is only documented for the header line and work area options).

System Variables

SY-TABIX contains the single record number of the new entry in itab1, or in the case of LINES OF itab2, the record number of the last record entered.

Cross-reference

See also COLLECT, DELETE, INSERT, LOOP, MODIFY, READ, SELECT, SORT, WRITE TO

Application Server

Definition

The "middle layer" in the SAP three-layer client-server-server architecture, where R/3 resides and runs (the application programs, ABAP/4 editor, and so on); below the SAPGUI Presentation Client and above the Database Server.

Cross-reference

See also Database server, Presentation Server, SAPGUI

Arithmetic functions for: (x) all numbers, (y) floating-point numbers, and (s) strings

Function	Description	Compliance
ABS(x)	Absolute value of x	[2.2] [3.0]
ACOS(y)	Arc-cosine of y, between 0 and Π	[3.0]

Arithmetic funcions for:

`ASIN( y )`	Arc-sine of y, between -Π/2 and Π/2	[3.0]
`ATAN( y )`	Arc-tangent of y, between -Π/2 and Π/2	[3.0]
`CEIL( x )`	Ceiling of x, that is, the smallest integer not less than x	[3.0]
`COS( y )`	Cosine of y, for y in radians	[2.2] [3.0]
`COSH( y )`	Hyperbolic cosine of y	[3.0]
`EXP( y )`	Exponential of y, that is, e**y for e = 2.7182818284590452	[2.2] [3.0]
`FLOOR( x )`	Floor of x, that is, the largest integer not greater than x	[3.0]
`FRAC( x )`	Fractional part of x, that is, the decimal portion of x	[3.0]
`INT( x )`	Use `TRUNC( x )`	[3.0]
`LOG( y )`	Logarithm base e of y, for y > 0	[2.2] [3.0]
`LOG10( y )`	Logarithm base 10 of y, for y > 0	[3.0]
`SIGN( x )`	Sign of x: 0 → 0; > 0 → 1; < 0 → -1	[3.0]
`SIN( y )`	Sine of y, for y in radians	[2.2] [3.0]
`SINH( y )`	Hyperbolic sine of y	[3.0]
`SQRT( y )`	Square root of y, for y >= 0	[2.2] [3.0]
`STRLEN( s )`	Number of characters in s, to the last non-blank character	[2.2] [3.0]
`TAN( y )`	Tangent of y, for y in radians	[3.0]
`TANH( y )`	Hyperbolic tangent of y	[3.0]
`TRUNC( x )`	Truncated x, that is, the integer portion of x	[3.0]

NOTE The arguments must be separated from the parentheses by spaces.

Arithmetic Operators

See Operators

ASIN

Compliance

| 3.0 |

Syntax

```
ASIN( y ).
```

Definition

Arc-sine of floating point number y, for y between -1 and +1, and
ASIN(y) between $-\Pi/2$ and $\Pi/2$.

Cross-reference

See also Arithmetic functions

ASSIGN

Compliance

| 2.2 | 3.0 |

Syntax

```
ASSIGN
{ [LOCAL COPY OF] {f1[+p1][(w1)] | (f2) }
| COMPONENT f3 OF STRUCTURE array1}
TO <fs> [TYPE t1] [DECIMALS d1].
```

definition

Points the field symbol $\langle fs \rangle$ to the field $f1$ or, for indirect addressing, to the field whose **name** is stored in the field $f2$. Parameter $p1$ may be a literal or variable offset; $w1$ may be a literal or variable width; if $p1 + w1$ is greater than the width of $f1$, then $\langle fs \rangle$ will point to the unde-fined bytes beyond the end of $f1$; to avoid this use "*" for $w1$.

LOCAL COPY OF f in a subroutine (FORM) creates a local copy of the global variable f and points the local field symbol to it.

COMPONENT $f3$ OF STRUCTURE $array1$ points the field symbol <fs> to element f3 of $array1$; if f3 is TYPE C, then it is treated as the name of the element in the array; otherwise, it is treated as the index of the desired element in the array.

TYPE $t1$ assigns TYPE $t1$ to the field symbol at runtime, $\langle fs \rangle$ defaults to the type of the assigned field otherwise.

DECIMALS $d1$ only applies to TYPE P.

System variables

SY-SUBRC	Description
0	the field was successfully assigned (for the indirect addressing case only)
>0	otherwise

AT fieldgroup1

Compliance

| 2.2 | 3.0 |

Syntax

AT fieldgroup1 [WITH fieldgroup2]. ... ENDAT.

Definition

Condition in a LOOP-ENDLOOP on a sorted extracted dataset that is true when the current record was created by the EXTRACT on fieldgroup1; WITH fieldgroup2 is true when the current record was created by the EXTRACT on fieldgroup1 and the immediately following record was created by the EXTRACT on fieldgroup2.

Cross-reference

See also EXTRACT, FIELD-GROUPS

AT END

Compliance

2.2   3.0

Syntax

AT END OF f1. ... ENDAT.

Definition

Condition in a LOOP-ENDLOOP on a sorted itab or a sorted extracted dataset that is true when the value of f1 or one of the fields to the left of f1 will change at the next record; also true at the last record. Within this AT...ENDAT code block, all fields in the header line to the right of f1 are filled with '*'. In an extracted dataset, f1 must be in the sort key. Don't use this command if the loop includes a FROM, TO, or WHERE statement.

Cross-reference

See also CNT(), SUM, SUM()

AT FIRST

Compliance

2.2   3.0

Syntax

```
AT FIRST...ENDAT.
```

Definition

Condition in a `LOOP-ENDLOOP` on an `itab` or an extracted dataset that is true during the first iteration. Within this `AT...ENDAT` code block, the header line does **not** contain table data. Don't use this command if the loop includes a `FROM`, `TO`, or `WHERE` statement.

Cross-reference

See also `SUM`

AT LAST

Compliance

 2.2 **3.0**

Syntax

```
AT LAST...ENDAT.
```

Definition

Condition in a `LOOP-ENDLOOP` on an itab or an extracted dataset that is true during the last iteration. Within this `AT...ENDAT` code block, the header line does **not** contain table data. Don't use this command if the loop includes a `FROM`, `TO`, or `WHERE` statement.

Cross-reference

See also `CNT()`, `SUM`, `SUM()`

AT LINE-SELECTION

Compliance

Syntax

```
AT LINE-SELECTION.
```

Definition

Event triggered by a selection (F2 or double-click with the cursor on a valid line) in an interactive report. A valid line is one created by statements such as `WRITE`, `ULINE`, or `SKIP`. Fields stored in the `HIDE` area are updated to the values of the selected line.

System variables

Field Name	Description
Runtime	
SY-TITLE	Title of report from attributes or text fields
List Generation	
SY-COLNO	Current column in list
SY-LINCT	Page length in list lines (from `REPORT`)
SY-LINNO	Current line in list
SY-LINSZ	Page width in columns (from `REPORT`)
SY-PAGNO	Current page in list
SY-SCOLS	Number of columns in window
SY-SROWS	Number of lines in window
Interactive Reporting	
SY-CPAGE	Current page number
SY-CUCOL	Cursor position (column) on-screen
SY-CUROW	Cursor position (line) on-screen
SY-LILLI	Number of selected list line

Field Name	Description
Interactive Reporting	
SY-LISEL	Contents of the selected line as a string
SY-LISTI	Index of selected list (0=base, 1=detail #1 etc.)
SY-LSIND	Index of displayed list (0=base, 1=detail #1 etc.)
SY-LSTAT	Status information for each list level
SY-MSGLI	Contents of the message line (line 23)
SY-STACO	Number of first displayed column
SY-STARO	Number of first displayed line on this page
SY-UCOMM	Command field function entry

Cross-reference

See also OKCODES

AT NEW

Compliance

 2.2 3.0

Syntax

```
AT NEW f1. ... ENDAT.
```

Definition

Condition in a LOOP-ENDLOOP on a sorted itab or a sorted extracted dataset that is true when the value of f1 or one of the fields to the left of f1 has just changed; also true at the first record if the first record value of f1 differs from that of the header line. Within this AT...ENDAT code block, all fields in the header line to the right of f1 are filled with '*'. In an extracted dataset, f1 must be in the sort key. Don't use this command if the loop includes a FROM, TO, or WHERE statement.

Cross-reference

See also SUM

AT PFnn

Compliance

Syntax

```
AT PFnn.
```

Definition

Event triggered by function key nn. Since function key assignments aren't fixed, your program may be more stable if you use AT
USER-COMMAND. The HIDE area fields and the system fields are updated as described in AT LINE-SELECTION.

AT SELECTION-SCREEN

Compliance

| 2.2 | 3.0 | for the main command

| 3.0 | for options marked with [3.0]

Syntax

```
AT SELECTION-SCREEN

[ ON ps

| ON END OF s
```

```
| ON VALUE REQUEST FOR ps_lmts [3.0]

| ON HELP REQUEST FOR ps_lmts [3.0]

| ON RADIOBUTTON GROUP r [3.0]

| ON BLOCK b [3.0]

| OUTPUT]. [3.0]
```

Definition

Events triggered in the selection screen of the program's Logical Database, in the order in which their corresponding object-creation statements (that is, PARAMETERS, SELECT-OPTIONS, SELECTION-SCREEN) appear in the code except as mentioned below. Issuing an "E"-type message in the event's code block returns focus to the selection screen and the offending field.

OUTPUT is triggered at the PBO, before the selection screen is displayed.

The next two events are triggered while in the screen. Variable ps_lmts is either the name of a parameter or the name of a select-option concatenated with "-HIGH" or "-LOW" to identify the subject field; these events can provide specialized choices or help.

ON VALUE REQUEST FOR ps_lmts is triggered if the user presses F4 (*Possible entries*) while the cursor is in the field or clicks the button beside the field; R/3 processes this block instead of displaying a check table or the Dictionary field values.

ON HELP REQUEST FOR ps_lmts is triggered if user presses F1 (*Help*) while the cursor is in the field; R/3 processes this block instead of displaying a check table or the Dictionary field documentation.

The remaining events are triggered after the PAI completes: They are processed in the order in which the PARAMETER, SELECT-OPTION, and SELECTION-SCREEN END OF BLOCK commands appear in the selection screen definition, followed by the basic event.

ON ps is triggered if the user completed PARAMETER ps or SELECT-OPTION ps;

ON END OF s is triggered if the user filled in the ranges for SELECT-OPTION s;

ON RADIOBUTTON GROUP r is triggered if the user selected a radiobutton in group r;

ON BLOCK b is triggered when all objects defined in block b have been completed;

Finally, the basic event AT SELECTION-SCREEN is triggered after the others are complete.

Cross-reference

See also MESSAGE, PARAMETERS, SELECT-OPTIONS

AT USER-COMMAND

Compliance

2.2   3.0

Syntax

AT USER-COMMAND.

Definition

Event triggered by all user commands defined in the Menu Painter; the value of the triggered code is available in SY-UCOMM for use in a CASE statement. Several system commands are trapped and processed by R/3, so they don't trigger this event, these include: the scroll functions P... and the command field entries /... and %..., PICK, PFn, PRI (print), BACK, RW (Rollback Work, that is, cancel). The HIDE area fields and the system fields are updated as described in AT LINE-SELECTION.

Cross-reference

See also OKCODES

ATAN

Compliance

3.0

Syntax

ATAN(y).

Definition

Arc-tangent of floating point number y, for ATAN(y) between -Π/2 and Π/2.

Cross-reference

See also Arithmetic functions

Attributes of fields, itabs, and lists

See DESCRIBE...

AUTHORITY-CHECK

Compliance

2.2   3.0

Syntax

AUTHORITY-CHECK OBJECT objectname

ID f1 FIELD v1

```
. . . .

ID fn FIELD vn.
```

Definition

Tests whether the user has access to the named authorization object and returns SY-SUBRC = 0 if the user has the authorization. Each authorization check object is defined with up to ten specific fields, `f1—fn`, referred to as IDs; the `AUTHORITY-CHECK` statement must specify each such field, and provide each with either a required value or the null test value `DUMMY`. The user must have a matching value to every non-`DUMMY` field in user's authorization profiles in order to be authorized access to `objectname`; those matching values need not all be in the same profile. Authorization objects and their required fields may be viewed in transaction /SU21. The user can view his or her own most recent authorization failure in transaction /SU56. For an authorization test that controls the entire program, you may limit access from transaction /SE38 in *Attributes by filling in <Authorization Group> with a value that matches the profile of the permitted users.

System variables

SY-SUBRC	Description
0	User is authorized access to objectname
4	User is NOT authorized access to objectname
8	Too many parameters
12	Object name not in user master control record
16	No profile in user master control record
24	Field names don't match those of objectname
>26	User master record has incorrect structure

BACK

Compliance

| 2.2 | | 3.0 |

Syntax

BACK.

Definition

Moves the cursor up to first line of the top-of-page area in the TOP-OF-PAGE code block. In the list generation loop and in the END-OF-PAGE code block, moves the cursor up to first line of the list. If used in an END-OF-PAGE called by a RESERVE statement, then it moves the cursor to the top of the end-of-page area.

Cross-reference

See also RESERVE

Batch Data Communications (BDC)

A "BDC session" or "Batch Input session" provides a means for bringing external data from a sequential file into the SAP database, using a defined transaction: Declare an itab LIKE BDCDATA then loop (read a sequential file record, populate itab, call a function that walks the transaction screens using the itab contents). BDCDATA is an SAP library structure. You must **thoroughly** understand the transaction before you can code the populating of itab.

See Part X for an example of a BDC session.

Bell

There's no `BELL`, `BEEP`, or `SOUND` command documented for ABAP/4.

BINARY SEARCH

See `READ TABLE` itab.

Boolean expressions

See Conditions, Operators.

BT

Relational operator "between"—see Operators.

BREAK-POINT

Compliance

| 2.2 | 3.0 |

Syntax

`BREAK-POINT.`

Definition

Halts the running program at this command and starts debugging mode. Since the debugger normally issues a `COMMIT WORK` that clears table cursors, don't insert a `BREAK-POINT` in a `SELECT...ENDSELECT` loop.

CA

String comparison operator "Contains At least one character from"—see Operators.

Call a program

Call another ABAP/4 program or report

See SUBMIT

Call an operating system (that is, UNIX or Windows NT) program on the application server

See OPEN DATASET...FILTER

CALL CUSTOMER-FUNCTION

Compliance

 2.2 3.0

Syntax

```
CALL CUSTOMER-FUNCTION f1.
```

Definition

Call a function written by the user in a user exit of an SAP program; f1 may be up to 3 characters long; the function name will be EXIT_ + the SAP module pool name + f1.

Example

If f1 = '001' and the module pool name is 'SAPMABCD', then the function module name is 'EXIT_SAPMABCD_001'

CALL DIALOG

Compliance

2.2 **3.0** for the main command

3.0 for options marked with [3.0]

Syntax

```
CALL DIALOG dcode

[AND SKIP FIRST SCREEN]

[EXPORTING f1 [FROM g1]

  . . .

  fn [FROM gn]]

[IMPORTING f1 [TO g1]

  . . .

  fn [TO gn]]

[USING itab MODE mode]. [3.0]
```

Definition

Calls the dialog module `dcode`; used similar to `CALL TRANSACTION` strictly in batch processes. Use transaction /SE35 to find dialog modules.

EXPORTING `f1`—the arguments (fields, structures, and itabs) passed to `dcode`;

FROM `g1`—the calling program's names for those arguments if different from `dcode`'s names;

IMPORTING `f1`—the arguments (fields, structures, and itabs) returned from `dcode`;

TO `g1`—the calling program's names for those arguments if different from `dcode`'s names;

The remaining parameters are defined in CALL TRANSACTION.

To depart from the dialog module, use the command LEAVE PRO-GRAM. A called dialog module will not process update requests, therefore, the calling program must explicitly or implicitly issue a COMMIT WORK after the dialog module completes.

Cross-reference

See also CALL FUNCTION, CALL TRANSACTION, SUBMIT

CALL FUNCTION

Compliance

2.2 **3.0** for the main command

3.0 for options marked with [3.0]

Syntax

CALL FUNCTION fmod [IN {UPDATE | BACKGROUND [3.0] } TASK]

[DESTINATION 'remote system name'

[STARTING NEW TASK f 'task name

[PERFORMING 'formname' ON END OF TASK]]]

EXPORTING f1 = a1 f2 = 'string'

IMPORTING f3 = a3 f4 = a4

CHANGING f5 = a5 [3.0]

TABLES   tab = itab (passed by reference)

EXCEPTIONS   e1 = subrc1 e2 = subrc2

    . . . .

Definition

Invokes a library function module.

NOTE   To insert the call in your program, use *[Pattern* [3.0] or *{Edit {Insert statement;*.

Use DESTINATION to issue a synchronous remote function call (RFC).

Use STARTING NEW TASK to make the RFC asynchronous.

IN UPDATE TASK sends the change requests to the Update Work process to hand off the work load from the Dialog Work process.

IN BACKGROUND TASK sets up to execute the function in another work process at the next COMMIT WORK.

PERFORMING 'formname' ON END OF TASK see discussion in RECEIVE RESULTS.

EXPORTING passes arguments (fields, structures, and itabs) by name from the calling program to the function module.

IMPORTING returns arguments back to the calling program from the function module.

CHANGING passes arguments from the calling program to the function module and returns the changed values to the calling program.

TABLES points to itabs; the table names must be declared in the function.

EXCEPTIONS lists the exceptions the calling program should be prepared to handle, and the return value for each; SY-SUBRC contains the value assigned to the exception returned.

Cross-reference

See also CALL DIALOG, CALL TRANSACTION, RECEIVE RESULTS, SUBMIT

CALL METHOD

Compliance

3.0

Syntax

```
CALL METHOD OF obj1 method1 [= f1] [NO FLUSH] [EX-
PORTING #1=f2 [#2=f3...]].
```

Definition

Calls a method of an external (OLE2) object; optionally assigns the method's return value to f1.

NO FLUSH continues OLE2 bundling even if the next statement isn't an OLE2 command.

EXPORTING passes field values f2... to the method's positional parameters #1....

Cross-reference

See also CREATE OBJECT, FREE OBJECT, GET PROPERTY, SET PROPERTY

CALL SCREEN

Compliance

 2.2   3.0

Syntax

```
CALL SCREEN scr

[STARTING AT c1 r1

[ENDING AT c2 r2]].
```

Definition

Displays screen scr, STARTING AT c1 r1—displays a modal dialog box with the upper-left corner at column c1, row r1. ENDING AT c2 r2—places the lower-right corner of the modal dialog box at column c2, row r2. If ENDING AT is not specified, the lower-right position will be determined by the size of scr.

To leave this screen, use `LEAVE TO SCREEN` 0 [3.0] or `SET SCREEN` 0. and `LEAVE SCREEN`.

Table cursors are cleared by `COMMIT WORK`, which is invoked by `CALL SCREEN`, so it shouldn't be used in a `SELECT... ENDSELECT` loop.

Cross-reference

See also `LEAVE SCREEN, SET SCREEN, WINDOW`

CALL TRANSACTION

Compliance

Syntax

```
CALL TRANSACTION tcode
        [AND SKIP FIRST SCREEN]
        USING bdc_table
        [MODE <display mode>]
        [UPDATE <update mode>].
```

Definition

Starts the transaction `tcode` for a Batch Data Communications (BDC) session. `AND SKIP FIRST SCREEN` attempts to process the first screen in the background by using SAP/GPA memory objects previously defined as PIDs or with `SET PARAMETER`. To depart from the transaction, use the command `LEAVE PROGRAM`. See Part V for lists of transaction codes.

Table 1.1   Parameters for Call Transaction

Parameter	Description
MODE	
A	Displays all steps (default)
E	Displays errors only
N	No display
UPDATE	
A	Continues processing of the caller while `tcode` proceeds in the background (default)
S	Waits for completion of `tcode` before re-starting the calling program

Table cursors are cleared by COMMIT WORK, which is invoked by CALL TRANSACTION, so CALL TRANSACTION shouldn't be used in a SELECT... ENDSELECT loop.

System variables

SY-SUBRC	Description
0	Successful
<1000	Error in dialog program
>1000	Error during batch input processing
SY-MSGID	Message ID
SY-MSGTY	Message type (E,I,W,S,A—see MESSAGE)
SY-MSGNO	Message number
SY-MSGV1	Message variable 1
SY-MSGV2	Message variable 2
SY-MSGV3	Message variable 3
SY-MSGV4	Message variable 4

Cross-reference

See also CALL DIALOG, CALL FUNCTION, SUBMIT

Case, upper and lower

See TRANSLATE

CASE

Compliance

Syntax

```
CASE field.

  WHEN value1.

    . . .

  WHEN value2.

    . . .

   [WHEN OTHERS].

    . . .

ENDCASE.
```

Definition

Finds the **first** WHEN clause whose value equals field, and executes the statements between that clause and the next WHEN or the ENDCASE, whichever it encounters first; any number of WHEN statements are allowed; typically field is a variable; value may be a variable or literal.

WHEN OTHERS is optional, only one is allowed and it must be the last WHEN clause; statements between WHEN OTHERS and ENDCASE are executed only if no other WHEN is true.

Cross-reference

See also DO, IF, WHILE

CEIL

Compliance

3.0

Syntax

```
CEIL( x ).
```

Definition

Ceiling of any number x, that is, the smallest integer not less than x.

Cross-reference

See also Arithmetic functions

CHAIN

Definition

Groups together several events for common processing in Flow Control.

See Flow Control

CHECK

Compliance

2.2   3.0

Syntax

```
CHECK {<condition> | f1 | SELECT-OPTIONS}.
```

Definition

Option 1. Continues processing with the next command if `<condition>` is true. If `<condition>` is false in a repetitive block (`DO`, `LOOP`, `SELECT`, `WHILE`), then it jumps to the end of the block for the next iteration. If `<condition>` is false in a non-repetitive block (`AT...`, `FORM`, `FUNCTION`, `MODULE`), then it terminates processing of the block.

Option 2. In a `GET` event, continues processing if the field `f1` corresponds to its `SELECT-OPTIONS` value. Otherwise, the event is terminated and subordinate tables are not processed.

Option 3. In a `GET` event, continues processing if all the fields correspond to their `SELECT-OPTIONS` values. Otherwise, the event is terminated and subordinate tables are not processed.

See Part X for an example of Logical Database processing (`GET` events).

Cross-reference

See also Condition, `CONTINUE`, `EXIT`, `LEAVE`, `REJECT`, `STOP`

CLEAR

Compliance

| **2.2** | **3.0** | for the main command |

| **3.0** | for options marked with [3.0] |

Syntax

```
CLEAR {f1 | itab }
[WITH {c | NULL}][3.0].
```

Definition

Option 1. Resets the contents of variable `f1` to the initial value of its type.

Option 2. If `itab` has a header line, it resets all the fields of the header line to their initial values; the table is unchanged. If `itab` has no header line it empties the table.

Option 3. Fills `f1` or `itab` to its declared length with the first byte of `c`.

Option 4. Fills `f1` or `itab` with the `NULL` value hex 00. Be careful: `NULL` is not a legal value for most TYPES.

Cross-reference

See also REFRESH, FREE

CLOSE CURSOR

Compliance

| 3.0 |

Syntax

CLOSE CURSOR cname.

Definition

Explicitly closes the database cursor `cname`.

Cross-reference

See also OPEN CURSOR, FETCH

CLOSE DATASET

Compliance

| 2.2 | | 3.0 |

Syntax

CLOSE DATASET filename.

Definition

Explicitly closes the sequential file on the application server. Open files are implicitly closed at every screen change.

Cross-reference

See also OPEN DATASET, READ DATASET, TRANSFER, DELETE DATASET

CNT

Compliance

| 2.2 | 3.0 |

Syntax

CNT(keyfield).

Definition

A system function available in LOOP structures on sorted dataset extracts where keyfield is in the sort key and is not a numeric field. Within the processing block AT LAST...ENDAT, CNT(keyfield) it returns the number of distinct values of keyfield in the extract. Within the processing block AT END OF testfield ... ENDAT, CNT(keyfield) it returns the number of distinct values of keyfield for the current value of testfield.

Cross-reference

See also AT END OF, AT LAST, CNT(), FIELD-GROUPS, LOOP, SUM()

CO

String comparison operator "Contains Only characters from"—see Operators.

COLLECT

Compliance

Syntax

```
COLLECT [wa INTO] itab.
```

Definition

Compares all header line (or work area `wa`) fields other than TYPES P,I, and F to their corresponding fields in `itab`. If the combination of values is not found, it appends the header line into `itab`. If the combination is found, it sums header line P, I, and F fields into the corresponding `itab` fields.

System variables

SY-TABIX contains the record number of the new or modified record.

Cross-reference

See also APPEND, INSERT, MODIFY, WRITE...TO

Color

Cross-reference

See FORMAT, PRINT-CONTROL

Comments

Definition

Comments are initiated by an asterisk (*) in the first column or by a double-quote (") in any column except in strings; they are terminated by the line break.

COMMIT

Compliance

| 2.2 | 3.0 | for the main command |

| 3.0 | for options marked with [3.0] |

Syntax

```
COMMIT WORK

    [AND WAIT [3.0]] .
```

Definition

Releases locks and table cursors and executes a database commit. Calls subroutines defined by PERFORM...ON COMMIT, completes any update requests specified by CALL FUNCTION...IN UPDATE TASK; and executes work started by CALL FUNCTION...IN BACKGROUND TASK. Committed work cannot be reversed by ROLLBACK WORK. AND WAIT halts the program until all the type V1 (U1) updates are complete. Type V2 (U2) updates will be executed in parallel with the re-started program.

Since table cursors are cleared by COMMIT WORK, and implicit work commits, those commands shouldn't be used in a SELECT...ENDSELECT loop or while using database cursors (that is, OPEN CURSOR and FETCH). Work is implicitly committed at end of CALL TRANSACTION programs and by the CALL SCREEN and BREAKPOINT commands.

Debug automatically issues a COMMIT WORK, so it alters the state when it enters the debug mode.

System variables

SY-SUBRC	Description
0	Successful
>0	Otherwise

Cross-reference

See also CALL DIALOG

COMMUNICATION

Compliance

Definition

Several forms used in the order shown to establish CPI-C communications between programs; the use of Remote Function Calls (RFCs) is preferred over this technique.

Syntax

COMMUNICATION INIT DESTINATION d1 ID id1

    [RETURNCODE rc1].

Requests connection with external system d1, assigns an ID number to the connection and assigns the return code to rc1.

COMMUNICATION ALLOCATE ID id1

    [RETURNCODE rc1].

Allocates resources; must immediately follow the INIT form.

COMMUNICATION ACCEPT ID id1

    [RETURNCODE rc1].

External system `d1` accepts the connection request.

`COMMUNICATION SEND ID id1 BUFFER f1`

    `[RETURNCODE rc1]`

    `[LENGTH w1]`.

Sends the contents of `f1` to the other system. `LENGTH w1` specifies the length of `f1` to send.

`COMMUNICATION RECEIVE ID id1 BUFFER f1`

    `DATAINFO d1` "returns information about the transmission;

    `STATUSINFO s1` "returns information about the program status

    `INCLUDE RSCPICDF` "to interpret the information in `d1` and `s1`

    `[RETURNCODE rc1]`

    `[LENGTH w1]` "specifies the length of `f1` to receive

    `[RECEIVED w2]` "the length of the data actually received

    `[HOLD]`.

Receives the data from the other system into `f1`. `HOLD` forces the program to wait for completion rather than rolling this out and performing other work; rolling out closes table cursors, so `SELECT` loops would crash.

`COMMUNICATION DEALLOCATE ID id1`

    `[RETURNCODE rc1]`.

Closes the connection and releases all resources.

COMPUTE

see Operators

CONCATENATE

Compliance

Syntax

```
CONCATENATE a b c... INTO d [SEPARATED BY
{e | SPACE}].
```

Definition

Concatenates any number of fields. Operands are treated as TYPE C without conversion. Trailing blanks are trimmed off before concatenation.

SEPARATED BY e inserts the string e between each of the operands.

SEPARATED BY SPACE inserts a space between each of the operands.

Example

```
DATA: st1(15) VALUE 'Texas',
    st2(15) VALUE 'California',
    st_list(32).
CONCATENATE st1 st2 INTO st_list SEPARATED BY ', '.
→   st_list contains 'Texas, California'
```

System variables

SY-SUBRC	Description
0	Successful
4	If the result is too long for d (in that case it is copied to the length of d)

CONCATENATE

To concatenate strings in Release 2.2, use the function module
`STRING_CONCATENATE`.

Cross-reference

See also the other string processing commands: `CONDENSE, OVERLAY,`
`REPLACE, SEARCH, SHIFT, SPLIT, STRLEN(), TRANSLATE`

CONDENSE

Compliance

Syntax

`CONDENSE string [NO-GAPS].`

Definition

Moves all "words" in `string` to the left until each is separated by one
space, or `[NO-GAPS]` with no spaces.

Example

```
DATA name(20) VALUE 'Que Computer       Books    '.
CONDENSE name   →          name contains 'Que
Computer Books'
CONDENSE name NO GAPS   →   name contains
'QueComputerBooks'
```

Cross-reference

See also the other string processing commands: `CONCATENATE,`
`OVERLAY, REPLACE, SEARCH, SHIFT, SPLIT, STRLEN(), TRANS-`
`LATE`

Condition

Compliance

| 2.2 | | 3.0 | for the main command |

| 3.0 | for options marked with [3.0] |

Definition

Binary (that is, TRUE/FALSE) conditions are used in the CHECK, ELSEIF, IF, WHERE, WHILE commands in any of the following forms. When they are used in a WHERE option, f1 is any field in the subject table, and vn is any literal value, variable, or constant.

Condition	Description
f1 [NOT] OP v1	OP is any of the relational operators EQ, NE, GT, GE, LT, LE (see Operators, Relational) or any of the string comparison operators CA, CO, CS, CP (see Operators, String). v1 may be SPACE.
[NOT] f1 IS INITIAL	May be used in CHECK, ELSEIF, IF, WHILE.
f1 [NOT] BETWEEN v1 AND v2	(Notice: this is **not** the logical AND)
f1 [NOT] LIKE v1 [ESCAPE s1]	v1 contains a search pattern where "_" replaces one character and "%" = any number of characters. A pattern character ("_" or "%") immediately following the escape character is interpreted literally.

continues

Condition

Condition	Description
`f1 [NOT] IN (v1, ..., vn)`	Notice no space after opening parenthesis.
`f1 [NOT] IN rtab`	Where `rtab` is an internal table like one created by `RANGES`. This condition is true for an empty `rtab`.
`f1 IS [NOT] NULL [3.0]`	`NULL` is hex 00; this is **not** the initial value for most TYPES.
`c1 AND c2`	The logical product of any two of these conditions; true if both `c1` and `c2` are true.
`c1 OR c2`	The logical sum of any two of these conditions; true if either `c1` or `c2` are true.
`(itab) [3.0]`	(Used for `SELECT` only.) `itab` contains the condition statements in its single TYPE C field no wider than 72 characters. The statements must be literal, containing no variables. Any of these above conditions may be included except `f1 IN rtab`. For example: `DATA: itab(72) OCCURS 10 WITH HEADER LINE.` `itab = 'COMPANY = '2001'''. APPEND itab.` `itab = 'COMPANY = ''2002''' . APPEND itab.`

Condition	Description
`cl AND (itab)` [3.0]	You may specify both hard-coded conditions and `itab` conditions.

Cross-reference

See also Operators

CONSTANTS

Compliance

| 3.0 |

Definition

Declares and assigns values to global and local constants.

Syntax

To declare a single constant:

`CONSTANTS fieldname[(length)]` "length only applies for TYPES C, N, P, and X

`[TYPE datatype]` "standard TYPES or TYPES defined in `TYPES` defaults to C (text)

`[LIKE otherfieldname]` "attributes only, not value

`[DECIMALS n]` "P TYPE only; n=0..14; defaults to 0 (integer)

`{VALUE [lit | const] | VALUE IS INITIAL }.` "const may be a system field such as SY-DATUM

To declare several constants:

`CONSTANTS: fieldname1[(length)]` options `VALUE val1.`

`fieldname2 VALUE val2.`

CONSTANTS

```
. . .  .
```

to declare complex constants (constant arrays):

```
CONSTANTS: BEGIN OF arrayname, [3.0]

    f1 TYPE t1 VALUE val1,

    f2 TYPE t2 VALUE val2,

  . . .

END OF arrayname.
```

    `<arrayname-f1>` returns the unpacked value for `f1`.

    `<arrayname>` returns all fields in a single packed string.

Cross-reference

See also DATA, LOCAL, STATICS, TABLES, TYPES

CONTINUE

Compliance

3.0

Syntax

CONTINUE.

Definition

Unconditionally jumps to top of the current repetitive processing block for next iteration; effective in DO, LOOP, SELECT, WHILE.

Cross-reference

See also CHECK, EXIT, LEAVE, REJECT, STOP

CONTROLS

Definition

Defines a runtime table control (a screen window for displaying itab lines).

Cross-reference

See also the online help and REFRESH CONTROL

CONVERT

Compliance

| 2.2 | 3.0 |

Syntax

```
CONVERT

{DATE d1 INTO INVERTED DATE d2

|INVERTED DATE d1 INTO DATE d2}.
```

Definition

Converts between special defined formats. INVERTED DATE is the nine's complement of the DATE internal representation YYYYMMDD, and therefore inverted dates sort in the reverse order to dates; this is rarely useful, as the DESCENDING option is available for sorting. For normal type conversions, see Part VIII, "Type Conversions."

Conversion

See Type Conversion

COS

Compliance

2.2 **3.0**

Syntax

COS(y).

Definition

Cosine of floating-point number y, for y in radians.

Cross-reference

See also Arithmetic functions

COSH

Compliance

3.0

Syntax

COSH(y).

Definition

Hyperbolic cosine of floating-point number y.

Cross-reference

See also Arithmetic functions

Country

See SET COUNTRY

CP

String comparison operator "Contains the Pattern"—see Operators.

CPI-C (Common Programming Interface—Communications)

Mechanism used by the Gateway Server for synchronous inter-program communications in R/3.

CREATE OBJECT

Compliance

3.0

Syntax

CREATE OBJECT obj1 class1 [LANGUAGE lng1].

Definition

Registers obj1 with SAP so subsequent OLE2 operations can be executed. LANGUAGE sets the language for the method and properties (default = English).

System variables

SY-SUBRC	Description
0	Successful
1	Communication error
2	Function call error
3	OLE API error
4	`obj1` not registered with SAP

Cross-reference

See also CALL METHOD, FREE OBJECT, GET PROPERTY, SET PROPERTY

CS

String comparison operator "Contains the String"—see Operators.

Cursor

For list processing, see GET CURSOR, SET CURSOR.

For database processing, see CLOSE CURSOR, FETCH, CLOSE CURSOR.

DATA

Compliance

2.2 **3.0** for the main command

3.0 for options marked with [3.0]

Definition

Declares variables and optionally assigns their attributes and starting values.

Syntax

To declare a single field:

DATA fieldname[(length)] "Length only applies for TYPES C, N, P, and X.

[TYPE datatype] "Standard TYPES or TYPES defined in TYPES; defaults to C (text).

[LIKE otherfieldname] "Attributes only, not value.

[DECIMALS n] "P TYPE only; n=0..14; defaults to 0 (integer)

[VALUE lit | const]. "Defaults to the initial value described in 'Initial values'; const may be a system field such as SY-DATUM.

To declare several fields, use the colon-and-commas construction:

DATA: fieldname1[(length)] options,

    fieldname2... .

To declare complex data TYPES:

DATA: BEGIN OF arrayname, f1 TYPE t1, f2 TYPE t2...END OF arrayname.

  <arrayname-f1> returns the unpacked value for f1.

  <arrayname> returns all fields in a single packed string.

or

DATA: array1 LIKE array2. "array2 was previously defined in DATA or TYPES, or

DATA: array1 TYPE LINE OF itabtype. "itabtype is a table TYPE created by TYPES, or

DATA: array1 LIKE LINE OF itab.

For an internal table with a header line:

DATA: itab LIKE dbtab OCCURS nocc WITH HEADER LINE. [3.0], or

DATA

DATA BEGIN OF itab OCCURS nocc.

    INCLUDE STRUCTURE struct1. "struct1 may be dbtab, itab or wa.

DATA END OF itab. or

NOTE   The LIKE construction is preferred over INCLUDE STRUCTURE [3.0].

DATA BEGIN OF itab OCCURS nocc.

      INCLUDE STRUCTURE struct1. "struct1 may be dbtab, itab or wa

      INCLUDE STRUCTURE struct2. "struct2 may be dbtab, itab or wa

DATA END OF itab.

or

DATA BEGIN OF itab OCCURS nocc.

    INCLUDE STRUCTURE struct1. "struct1 may be dbtab, itab or wa

DATA: fieldname1[(length)] options,

    fieldname2....

DATA END OF itab, or

DATA: BEGIN OF itab OCCURS nocc,

    f1 TYPE t1,

    . . .

    END OF itab., or

DATA: itab LIKE array OCCURS nocc WITH HEADER LINE., or

DATA: itab TYPE itabtype WITH HEADER LINE. "itabtype is a table TYPE created by TYPES, or

DATA: BEGIN OF itab OCCURS nocc,

    istruct LIKE dbtab,

```
END OF itab.
```

(Refer to these fields by: `itab-istruct-fieldname`).

For an internal table without a header line:

`DATA: itab LIKE array OCCURS nocc.`, or

`DATA: itab TYPE type1 OCCURS nocc.` "`type1` may be a standard or complex TYPE, or

`DATA: itab TYPE itabtype.` "`itabtype` is a table TYPE created by `TYPES`.

The `OCCURS` value `nocc` must be a literal number; zero is allowed. Its value affects only the command `APPEND...SORTED BY`.

Cross-reference

See also `CONSTANTS, LOCAL, STATICS, TABLES, TYPES`

Database Server

Definition

The "bottom layer" in the SAP three-layer client-server-server architecture, where the SQL database resides; below the SAPGUI Presentation Client and the Application Server.

Cross-reference

See also Application server, Presentation server, SAPGUI

date

Definition

Date TYPE variables are stored as packed fields interpreted as the number of days since 01/01/0001. Addition and subtraction are supported between dates and P and I numbers.

Cross-reference

See also CONVERT, Part II, System Fields for the system field SY-DATUM

dbtab

Definition

A table maintained by SAP in the underlying database that may contain system information, master data, lookup information, or transaction data. The commands that affect dbtabs include: DELETE, DESCRIBE DISTANCE, FREE, GET, INSERT, MODIFY, SELECT, TABLES, UPDATE.

Cross-reference

See also itab, table types

debug

Definition

/H in the command field starts the debug mode ("Hoppel" is German slang for debug). Debug automatically issues a COMMIT WORK, so it alters the program state when it starts.

Cross-reference

See also BREAK-POINT and transactions /ST05 (SQL Trace), /SE30 (ABAP/4 Trace), /SDBE (Explain SQL)

DEFINE

Compliance

| 2.2 | 3.0 |

Syntax

```
DEFINE macroname.
```

    ... "ABAP/4 statements

    ... "may include up to nine parameters and1..and9 defined by calling arguments

```
END-OF-DEFINITION.
```

Definition

Creates a macro. The macro is called by using its name, followed by any required arguments; it must be defined before it is called. Macros may be nested, but they may not recurse.

Example

```
DATA: title(32) VALUE 'Report Header',
      colhdr(72).
colhdr = 'Index     Name      Description    Date'.
DEFINE writeheader.
    ULINE.
    WRITE: SY-DATUM, and1 CENTERED, SY-UNAME, /,
and2.
END-OF-DEFINITION.
...
WRITE 'Before macro'.
writeheader title colhdr.
WRITE: / 'After macro'.

→

Before macro
-----------------------------------------------------
-----------------------
05/06/1997              Report Header              USER01

Index     Name      Description    Date
After macro
```

DELETE ADJACENT DUPLICATES

Compliance

| 3.0 |

Syntax

```
DELETE ADJACENT DUPLICATES FROM itab

[COMPARING { f1 f2... | ALL FIELDS} ].
```

Definition

If there are consecutive records in `itab` whose primary keys are equal, this command will delete the second and subsequent records. The primary key of an `itab` is the concatenation of all non-F I P fields. COMPARING f1 f2... deletes adjacent records if their listed field values are equal. COMPARING ALL FIELDS deletes adjacent records if their entire records are equal. This command is especially useful after a SORT [DESCENDING] on `itab`.

System variables

SY-SUBRC	Description
0	At least one record is deleted
>0	Otherwise

DELETE itab

Compliance

| 2.2 | | 3.0 |

Syntax

```
DELETE itab
```

```
[INDEX ndx

| WHERE <condition>

| [FROM ndx1] [TO ndx2]].
```

Definition

Deletes the current record from `itab` in a `LOOP . . ENDLOOP` structure.

`INDEX ndx`—deletes record number `ndx` from `itab`.

`WHERE <condition>`—deletes records from `itab` that satisfy the condition.

`FROM ndx1`—starting deleting from record number `ndx1` where `ndx1 > 0`.

`TO ndx2`—deletes down to and including record number `ndx2` where `ndx2 >= ndx1`.

System variables

SY-SUBRC	Description
0	At least one record is deleted
>0	Otherwise

Cross-reference

See also `INSERT`, `MODIFY`

DELETE dbtab

Compliance

| 2.2 | 3.0 |

Syntax

`DELETE dbtab [FROM {wa | TABLE itab}].`

DELETE dbtab

Definition

Deletes one record from `dbtab` whose primary key matches that in the header line.

`FROM wa` deletes one record from `dbtab` whose primary key matches the left-most characters in the work area `wa` out to the length of the primary key; the structure of `wa` is ignored.

`FROM TABLE itab` deletes all records from `dbtab` whose primary keys match those of the left-most characters in **any record** of `itab` out to the length of the primary key; the structure of `itab` is ignored.

System Variables

SY-SUBRC	Description
0	At least one record was deleted or itab was empty
4	No primary key matched
SY-DBCNT	Contains the number of records deleted

DELETE FROM dbtab

Compliance

Syntax

`DELETE FROM dbtab WHERE <condition>.`

Definition

Deletes records from `dbtab` that satisfy the `WHERE` condition.

System variables

SY-SUBRC	Description
0	Successful
>0	Otherwise
SY-DBCNT	Contains the number of records deleted

Cross-reference

See also WHERE

DELETE DATASET

Compliance

2.2 3.0

Syntax

DELETE DATASET filename.

Definition

Deletes the named sequential file on the application server.

System variables

SY-SUBRC	Description
0	Successful
>0	Otherwise

Cross-reference

See also CLOSE DATASET, OPEN DATASET, READ DATASET,
TRANSFER

DELETE REPORT

Compliance

2.2 3.0

Syntax

DELETE REPORT rpt1.

Definition

Deletes the source code, attributes, textpool, and generated version of program `rpt1` (the documentation and variants are not deleted). The function module `RS_DELETE_PROGRAM` is the preferred way to delete a report.

System variables

SY-SUBRC	Description
0	The program was deleted
>0	Otherwise

Cross-reference

See also `DELETE TEXTPOOL`, `INSERT REPORT`, `READ REPORT`

DELETE TEXTPOOL

Compliance

Syntax

```
DELETE TEXTPOOL, rpt1 LANGUAGE {lng1 | *}.
```

Definition

Deletes the text elements for program `rpt1` in language `lng1`, or (*) in all languages. SY-LANGU contains the language selected at login.

Cross-reference

See also `INSERT TEXTPOOL`, `READ TEXTPOOL`, Text Elements

DEQUEUE

See ENQUEUE

DESCRIBE DISTANCE

Compliance

Syntax

DESCRIBE DISTANCE BETWEEN tab-f1 AND tab-f2 INTO
nchar.

Definition

Returns in nchar the number of characters between the beginning of
field f1 and the beginning of field f2 in table tab. tab may be a
dbtab, an itab, or an array.

DESCRIBE FIELD

Compliance

 for the main command

3.0 for options marked with [3.0]

Syntax

```
DESCRIBE FIELD f1
```

[LENGTH len] "Returns the length in len.

[OUTPUT-LENGTH len] "Returns the output-length in len*.

[DECIMALS n] "Returns the decimals in DATA declaration of this TYPE P field.

[EDIT MASK mask] "Returns the name of f1's Dictionary conversion routine prefixed by '=='.

[TYPE typ "Returns the TYPE in typ.

  [COMPONENTS n]] . [3.0] And if f1 is a structure, returns the number of components in n.

Definition

Returns the requested attributes about field f1. You must specify at least one attribute.

NOTE OUTPUT-LENGTH is the field length as it would be printed in a list; see its Domain definition. For example, a TYPE P field's output length may be twice its length.

DESCRIBE LIST

Compliance

Syntax

```
DESCRIBE LIST
```

[NUMBER OF {LINES ln1 "Returns the number of lines in the current list in ln1.

| PAGES p1 } "Returns the number of pages in the current list in p1.

| `LINE` ln2 `PAGE` p2 "Returns the page number in p2 of line ln2.

| `PAGE` p3 "Returns the following attributes of page p3 : .

[`INDEX` ndx1] "List level of the page.

[`LINE-SIZE` w1] "Line width for the page.

[`LINE-COUNT` r1] "Maximum number of lines allowed.

[`LINES` n1] "Number of lines written on the page.

[`FIRST-LINE` n2] "Line number of first line.

[`TOP-LINES` n3] "Number of lines in page header "(title, column headers and TOP-OF-PAGE).

[`TITLE-LINES` n4] "Number of title lines.

[`HEAD-LINES` n5] "Number of column header lines.

[`END-LINES` n6]] "Number of lines reserved for end of page processing.

[`INDEX` ndx1] . "Returns the current list level.

Definition

Returns the selected information about the current list (report).

System variables

SY-SUBRC	Description
0	Successful
>0	Index level doesn't exists

DESCRIBE TABLE

Compliance

2.2 3.0

Syntax

```
DESCRIBE TABLE itab [LINES nlin] [OCCURS noct].
```

Definition

LINES returns in the field `nlin` the current number of records in `itab`. The system field SY-TFILL also contains the number after this command is executed.

OCCURS returns in the field `nocc` the OCCURS value of `itab`. The system field SY-TOCCU also contains the number after this command is executed. (Note: R/3 may change the OCCURS value during execution from the DATA value.)

You must specify at least one attribute.

Dispatcher

The dispatcher is a central controller in R/3 that continuously routes work sessions among the appropriate Work processes established in the instance.

See Instance, Work processes

DIV

Integer division—see Operators.

DIVIDE

Compliance

| 2.2 | 3.0 |

Syntax

```
DIVIDE a BY b.
```

Definition

Equivalent to $a = a / b$. Division by 0 is illegal, except that $0 / 0 = 0$. Non-numeric fields are converted; see "Type Conversions," Part VIII, for conversion information.

Cross-reference

See also ADD, MULTIPLY, SUBTRACT

DIVIDE-CORRESPONDING

Compliance

Syntax

```
DIVIDE-CORRESPONDING array1 TO array2.
```

Definition

If array1 and array2 are structured work areas such as header lines, then this command divides **like-named** fields in array1 and array2. It's equivalent to:

```
DIVIDE array1-key1 BY array2-key1.
DIVIDE array1-key2 BY array2-key2.
. . .
```

Cross-reference

See also ADD-CORRESPONDING, MULTIPLY-CORRESPONDING, SUBTRACT-CORRESPONDING

DO

Compliance

Syntax

```
DO [n TIMES] [VARYING v1 FROM array1-fm NEXT ar-
ray1-fn].

...

ENDDO.
```

Definition

Loops n times or until terminated by EXIT or STOP. Changing n inside the loop doesn't affect the number of times the loop executes. VARYING steps the variable v1 in subsequent passes, see VARY for an example. DO-loops may be nested indefinitely.

CONTINUE unconditionally skips to the ENDDO for the next iteration. CHECK <condition> skips to ENDDO for the next iteration if the condition is false. EXIT terminates the loop; execution continues with the statement after ENDDO. STOP terminates the loop; execution continues with the event END-OF-SELECTION.

System variables

SY-INDEX contains the one-based current step for the current nest level; after the ENDDO, it is restored to its value before the DO.

Cross-reference

See also CASE, IF, LOOP, WHILE

DOWNLOAD

Definition

Function module to write an `itab` to a local disk file on the user's workstation. This function module presents a dialog box to enter filename and type (ASCII, BIN, Excel/DAT, spreadsheet/WK1). `WS_DOWNLOAD` is similar except filename and type are parameters rather than prompts.

NOTE To insert the call in your program, use *[Pattern* [3.0] or *{Edit {Insert statement.*

Cross-reference

See also `UPLOAD`, `WS_DOWNLOAD`, `WS_EXECUTE`, `WS_QUERY`, `WS_UPLOAD`

dynpros

"Dynamic Programs" are equivalent to user transaction screens, associated programs, and grqphical screen definition.

EDITOR-CALL

Compliance

| 2.2 | 3.0 |

Syntax

EDITOR-CALL FOR {itab [TITLE 'text string'] I REPORT rpt1 }

`[DISPLAY MODE] .`

Definition

Places the internal table `itab` or the program `rpt1` in the SAP Editor so the user may edit it. In `DISPLAY MODE` the user may only view it. The `itab` must contain only a TYPE C field whose record length is limited to 72 characters. The Save button, F11, saves changes and returns to the calling program, and the Return button, F3, closes the Editor without saving.

System variables

SY-SUBRC	Description
0	Changes were saved before leaving
>0	Otherwise

END-OF-PAGE

Compliance

Syntax

```
END-OF-PAGE.
```

Definition

Event triggered at the end of each basic and detailed list page if an end-of-page area is reserved by the `LINE-COUNT` parameter (in the `REPORT` statement or in a previous `NEW-PAGE` statement), or by a `RESERVE` statement. `END-OF-PAGE` is not triggered at the end of the list unless the line count is full. `NEW-PAGE` **does not** trigger this event.

Cross-reference

See also TOP-OF-PAGE

END-OF-SELECTION

Compliance

Syntax

END-OF-SELECTION.

Definition

Event triggered after all the Logical Database records have been processed, when the START-OF-SELECTION event completes if no Logical Database is in use, or by the STOP command.

Cross-reference

See also Events

ENQUEUE_OBJECTNAME...

Definition

A set of function modules used to lock objects. Locks are automatically
released at the end of the transaction; they can also be released by calling the matching DEQUEUE_OBJECTNAME... function module.

EQ

Relational operator "Equal"—see Operators.

Events

Definition

When any event is triggered, processes jumps to the first command following the Event statement and continues to the end of that code block. The code block is terminated by the next Event statement, the first FORM definition, or the end of the program.

Cross-reference

See also CHECK, STOP

Events in online transactions

```
AT LINE-SELECTION.

AT PFnn.

AT USER-COMMAND.

PROCESS AFTER OUTPUT.

PROCESS ON HELP-REQUEST.

PROCESS ON VALUE-REQUEST.

PROCESS BEFORE INPUT.
```

Events in reports and programs

```
AT SELECTION-SCREEN [ON p | ON s | OUTPUT].

END-OF-PAGE.

END-OF-SELECTION.

GET [LATE].

INITIALIZATION.

START-OF-SELECTION.

TOP-OF-PAGE [DURING LINE SELECTION].
```

The normal processing order in a program is:

- INITIALIZATION one time before the selection screen is displayed, then
- AT SELECTION-SCREEN OUTPUT every time before the selection screen is shown, then
- PARAMETERS, SELECT-OPTIONS and SELECTION-SCREEN commands, wherever they're located, then
- AT SELECTION-SCREEN ON {p | s} if user has specified the parameter p or select-option s, then
- AT SELECTION-SCREEN when the user accepts the screen, then
- The code between the REPORT statement and the first event statement, then
- START-OF-SELECTION, then
- If REPORT has a Logical Database assigned in the Attributes screen, the internal LDB reader steps through the Logical Database hierarchically, one record at a time, triggering the appropriate GET events as the records are available, then
- END-OF-SELECTION

EXEC SQL

Compliance

2.2 **3.0** for the main command

3.0 for options marked with [3.0]

Syntax

```
EXEC SQL [PERFORMING formname[3.0]] .

. . .

ENDEXEC .
```

Definition

Provides the ability to issue native SQL commands directly to the database. This is dangerous business in SAP because transaction data is sprinkled throughout many tables, not just posted in one place. Do it only if (1) it's absolutely necessary, and (2) you **really** know what you're doing.

PERFORMING calls the subroutine `formname` after each record retrieved by the SQL statement.

Cross-reference

See also EXIT FROM SQL, Open SQL

Execute a program

Execute another ABAP/4 program or report

See SUBMIT

Execute an operating system (that is, UNIX or Windows NT) program on the application server.

See OPEN DATASET...FILTER

EXIT

Compliance

| 2.2 | 3.0 | for the main command |

| 3.0 | for options marked with [3.0] |

Syntax

```
EXIT [FROM { STEP-LOOP | SQL[3.0]  } ] .
```

Definition

Terminates the processing blocks `AT. . .`, `AT. . .ENDAT`, `DO`, `END-OF-PAGE`, `FORM`, `FUNCTION`, `LOOP`, `MODULE`, `SELECT`, `TOP-OF-PAGE`, `WHILE`. Outside of those blocks it cancels report processing and displays whatever list had been generated to that point. See also `CHECK`, `CONTINUE`, `LEAVE`, `REJECT`, `STOP`.

`FROM STEP-LOOP` (in Flow Control) departs the current screen, ceases processing of the PBO, and skips the PAI. See also Flow Control.

`FROM SQL` departs the loop created by `EXEC SQL PERFORMING formname`.

EXP

Compliance

Syntax

```
EXP( y ) .
```

Definition

Exponential of floating-point number `y`, that is, $e**y$ for $e = 2.7182818284590452$.

Cross-reference

See also Arithmetic functions

EXPORT

Compliance

2.2   3.0

Syntax

```
EXPORT f1 [FROM g1] f2 [FROM g2]... TO MEMORY [ID
ident].
```

Definition

Stores in user-assigned memory the names and values of the listed data objects; the objects can be simple fields, records, table work areas, and internal tables. Each EXPORT to an ident (or to no ident) overwrites the previous such EXPORT. The data objects can be retrieved (using the names f1..) with IMPORT and the same ident. The user-assigned memory is released when the current call chain is completed. f1 FROM g1 stores the data object g1 under the name f1. ID associates the label ident with this group of objects.

EXTRACT

Compliance

2.2   2.2

Syntax

```
EXTRACT fg.
```

Definition

Temporarily stores in memory as a record the field group fg and its header. Records defined by different field groups can be interleaved.

The records can be sorted and then analyzed in a `LOOP` ... `ENDLOOP` structure.

Cross-reference

See also `CNT()`, `FIELD-GROUPS`, `INSERT`, `LOOP`, `SORT`, `SUM()`

FALSE

There's no logical TYPE in ABAP. Logical state is frequently represented by a 1-character `TYPE C` field. with its initial value ' ' or `SPACE` for `FALSE`, and 'X' for `TRUE`.

FETCH

Compliance

3.0

Syntax

`FETCH NEXT CURSOR cname INTO wa.`

Definition

Fills `wa` with the contents of the record identified by `cname`, then increments `cname`. `cname` must be of `TYPE CURSOR` and previously created with an `OPEN CURSOR` command.

`COMMIT WORK` clears table cursors, so any commands that invoke `COMMIT WORK` shouldn't be used before a `FETCH` command. Those commands include: `CALL SCREEN`, `CALL TRANSACTION`, `COMMIT WORK`, `BREAKPOINT`.

System variables

SY-SUBRC	Description
0	A line was read
>0	Otherwise
SY-DBCNT	Contains the number of lines read using cursor `cname`

Cross-reference

See also CLOSE CURSOR, OPEN CURSOR

Field names

See Names

FIELD-GROUPS

Compliance

Syntax

```
FIELD-GROUPS fg.
```

Definition

Declares the field group `fg`, which will be a set of fields selected from one or more tables. Assign the fields to `fg` by using INSERT. Fills by `fg` from the tables by using EXTRACT. Analyze the extracted dataset with LOOP ... ENDLOOP.

Cross-reference

See also AT...ENDAT, CNT(), EXTRACT, INSERT, LOOP, SORT, SUM()

FIELD-SYMBOLS

Compliance

| 2.2 | 3.0 |

Syntax

FIELD-SYMBOLS <fs> [STRUCTURE dbtab DEFAULT wa].

Definition

Declares the symbolic field <fs>. The program may then assign an actual field or pointer at runtime by using the ASSIGN command. STRUCTURE assigns the structure of dbtab to fs; refer to the elements as <fs>-fl and so forth. DEFAULT wa makes wa the initial assignment target of <fs>.

Cross-reference

See also Part III for an example, ASSIGN

FLOOR

Compliance

| 3.0 |

Syntax

FLOOR(x).

Definition

Floor of any number x, that is, the largest integer not greater than x, or the integer value of x.

Cross-reference

See also Arithmetic functions, FRAC, TRUNC

Flow Control

See CHAIN, EXIT FROM STEP-LOOP, MODULE, PROCESS...

FORM

Compliance

Syntax

FORM name

    [TABLES itab1 [STRUCTURE dbtab]] "(pass by reference)

  [USING

   [wa STRUCTURE dbtab] "(pass by reference)

   [f1 [TYPE t1]] "(pass by reference)

   [VALUE(f2) [LIKE v1]]] "(pass by value)

  [CHANGING f3] "(pass by reference; indicates subroutine output)

   [CHANGING VALUE(f4)]. "(pass by value and write the formal parameter back to the actual parameter on normal termination; the CHANGING VALUE in the called FORM statement must match a CHANGING attribute in the calling PERFORM)

. . .

```
ENDFORM.
```

Definition

Defines a subroutine. Parameters are optional, and its formal parameters must have matching actual parameters in the calling PERFORM statement. Formal parameters with TYPE or LIKE clauses must match their actual parameter TYPES. TABLES, USING, and CHANGING must appear in that order. You normally will pass parameters to the subroutine with USING and return them with CHANGING; you may pass parameters back and forth by using VALUE (being very careful of system fields SY-. .). You **must** place the source code for form definitions at the end of the program. Definitions may not nest (one FORM may not be defined inside another FORM definition) but calls may nest and recurse.

EXIT immediately terminates the subroutine normally and returns to the calling code. CHECK <condition> terminates normally if the condition is false. STOP unconditionally jumps to the event END-OF-SELECTION. An error message terminates the subroutine abnormally.

Scope

DATA, CONSTANTS, and TABLES declarations in the main program are global to that program, all its subroutines and all its INCLUDES.

DATA, CONSTANTS, and TABLES declarations in a subroutine are local to that subroutine and are initialized each call. Such fields are not available to subroutines that are called from the one in which they were declared.

STATICS declarations work exactly like DATA inside the subroutine except the values of the variables thus declared are retained between calls to the subroutine.

LOCAL declarations use the attributes and values of listed global variables within the subroutine and restore their original values upon returning from the subroutine.

FORMAT

Compliance

| 2.2 | | 3.0 | for the main command

| 3.0 | for options marked with [3.0]

Syntax

```
FORMAT]
```

{ COLOR {n | ON | OFF} "see below

| HOTSPOT {ON | OFF | var} "mouse cursor changes to point-ing hand in this field [3.0]

| INTENSIFIED {ON | OFF | var} "background only; pastel or saturated color

| INVERSE {ON | OFF | var} "foreground and background colors

| INPUT {ON | OFF | var} "permits entering data in line at this field

| RESET } . "returns all attributes to OFF

Definition

Sets or modifies only the screen output; printer output is affected by PRINT CONTROL. ON is the default, so INPUT ON is the same as IN-PUT. var is a TYPE I field that R/3 interprets as off if it's equal to 0 and on if it's greater than 0. FORMAT commands take affect with the next WRITE or NEW-LINE. Each new program event resets COLOR, INTEN-SIFIED, INVERSE, and INPUT. Use READ LINE to accept the data entered in INPUT fields.

Table 1.2   Color Parameters

Value of N	Color
{0 | OFF | col_background}	GUI-specific
{1 | col_heading}	Grayish blue
{2 | col_normal}	Bright grey
{3 | col_total}	Yellow
{4 | col_key}	Bluish green
{5 | col_positive}	Green
{6 | col_negative}	Red
{7 | col_group}	Violet

Cross-reference

See also PRINT CONTROL, WRITE

formfeed

see NEW-PAGE

FRAC

Compliance

3.0

Syntax

FRAC(x).

Definition

Fractional part of any number x, that is, the decimal portion of x.

Cross-reference

See also Arithmetic functions, FLOOR

FREE

Compliance

| 2.2 | 3.0 | for the main command |

| 3.0 | for options marked with [3.0] |

Syntax

`FREE {f [3.0] | itab | dbtab | MEMORY [ID ident]}.`

Definition

Clears data object f to its initial value and releases allocated resources.

Empties itab and frees the memory allocated; it remains defined and can be reused. If itab has a header line, the header line remains unchanged.

Releases the work area for dbtab; it remains defined and can be reused.

Releases memory allocated for EXPORT TO MEMORY.

Cross-reference

See also CLEAR, REFRESH

FREE OBJECT

Compliance

| 3.0 |

Syntax

```
FREE OBJECT obj1.
```

Definition

Releases the memory allocated to the OLE2 object obj1.

System variables

SY-SUBRC	Description
0	The memory was successfully released
1	An error in the communication with the SAPGUI
2	An error in the function call in the SAPGUI

Cross-reference

See also CALL METHOD, CREATE OBJECT, GET PROPERTY, SET PROPERTY

FUNCTION

Compliance

Syntax

```
FUNCTION f1.
```

Definition

The beginning of the function module definition.

Cross-reference

See also function group, function module, FUNCTION-POOL

Function group

Definition

To create a function groups, use transaction *SE37* and follow the menu path *{Goto {Function groups {Create group <name* = 'Zxxx'. R/3 creates a program shell named SAPLZxxx containing an INCLUDE named LZxxxTOP, which is headed by the FUNCTION-POOL statement that is designated for global data for the function group.

Function module

Definition

To create a function module, use transaction *SE37* and select *<name* = 'Z_*' [Create ...   (name is limited to 30 letters and the underscore). R/3 creates an INCLUDE in the function module SAPLZxxx, which is headed by the statement FUNCTION name. The function module is invoked by CALL FUNCTION.

FUNCTION-POOL

Compliance

| 2.2 | 3.0 |

Syntax

FUNCTION-POOL fpl.

Definition

The header statement of source code of the function modules in the function group.

Cross-reference

See also function module, PROGRAM, REPORT

Gateway server—An instance of the SAP system

Cross-reference

See also Instance

GE

Relational operator "Greater Than or Equal"—see Operators.

GET CURSOR FIELD

Compliance

2.2   3.0

Syntax

```
GET CURSOR FIELD fl [LENGTH len] [LINE lin] [OFFSET
off] [VALUE val].
```

Definition

In list processing, returns in fl the global field name where the cursor is currently located. It optionally returns the additional information: len is the output length of the field; lin is the absolute line number in the list (SY-LILLI); off is the zero-based position of the cursor in the field; val is the screen contents of the value of the field (shown as characters). If the cursor is located on a screen literal, local variable or VALUE parameter of a subroutine, this command will return `f1 = SPACE` and `val = 0`.

System variables

SY-SUBRC	Description
0	The cursor is positioned on a field
>0	Otherwise

Cross-reference

See also `SET CURSOR`

GET CURSOR LINE

Compliance

| 3.0 |

Syntax

```
GET CURSOR LINE lin [LENGTH len] [OFFSET off]
[VALUE val].
```

Definition

In list processing, returns in `lin` the absolute line number in the list (SY-LILLI) where the cursor is currently located. It optionally returns the additional information: `len` is the output length of the line (`LINE-SIZE`); `off` is the zero-based position of the cursor in the list line; `val` is the screen contents of the value of the line as characters (doesn't include the `HIDE` fields).

System variables

SY-SUBRC	Description
0	The cursor is positioned on a list line
>0	Otherwise

Cross-reference

See also SET CURSOR

GET

Compliance

Syntax

GET dbtab [LATE].

Definition

Logical Database event triggered by the internal Logical Database reader program: the next record of dbtab is available. The LATE event is triggered when the record in dbtab is going to change (that is, all lower level tables have been processed).

Cross-reference

See also Part X for an example, REJECT, ON CHANGE OF

GET PARAMETER ID

Compliance

Syntax

```
GET PARAMETER ID key FIELD f.
```

Definition

Assigns to f the value of PID key in the user's SPA/GPA memory area.

System variables

SY-SUBRC	Description
0	A value was found for PID key
>0	Otherwise

Cross-reference

See also SET PARAMETER ID

GET PROPERTY

Compliance

3.0

Syntax

```
GET PROPERTY OF obj1 p1 = f1 [NO FLUSH].
```

Definition

Assigns to field f1 attribute p1 of the OLE2 object obj1. NO FLUSH continues OLE2 bundling even if the next statement isn't an OLE2 command.

System variables

SY-SUBRC	Description
0	All OLE2 commands in the bundle were successful
1	Communication error, described in SY-MSGL1
2	Method call error, described in dialog box
3	Property set up error, described in dialog box
4	Property read error, described in dialog box

Cross-reference

See also CALL METHOD, CREATE OBJECT, FREE OBJECT, SET PROPERTY

GET RUN TIME

Compliance

Syntax

GET RUN TIME FIELD f.

Definition

Assigns to f the time in microseconds since the first time this command was issued. The variable f must be TYPE I. Use transaction *ISE30* to analyze complex runtime processes.

GET TIME

Compliance

Syntax

`GET TIME [FIELD f1].`

Definition

Resets SY-DATUM and SY-UZEIT to current date and time. `FIELD f1` assigns the time in SY-UZEIT to `f1` without changing SY-UZEIT.

GOTO

There is no GOTO-type command, and there are no line labels in ABAP/4.

GPA

See `GET PARAMETER`, SPA/GPA Memory Area.

GT

Relational operator "Greater Than"—see Operators.

Header line

A structured work area with the same structure as the associated table. Typically, it has the same name as the table. Non-table commands such as MOVE refer to the header line; table commands such as APPEND refer to the table and sometimes to the header line. The notation tablename[] always refers to the table.

Cross-reference

See also dbtab, itab, Work area

HIDE

Compliance

Syntax

HIDE f1 [f2...].

Definition

Stores f1 [f2...] in a "hidden" (that is, off-screen) area linked to the list lines created by an immediately-preceding WRITE statement. When an on-screen line is selected, the values in that line are assigned to the variables from which they came, including the hidden fields and the header line. HIDE is generally used to store key fields, but there is no restriction to what it can store. The hidden field(s) need not have been included in the preceding WRITE statement.

IF

Compliance

Syntax

```
IF <condition1>.

   ..

[ELSEIF <condition2>.

   ..]

[ELSE.

   ..]

ENDIF.
```

Definition

Finds the first true condition and executes the statements between that clause and the next ELSEIF, ELSE, or ENDIF, whichever it encounters first. Any number of ELSEIF statements are allowed. ELSE is optional and must follow the last ELSEIF statements. IF statements may be nested without limit.

Cross-reference

See also CASE, Condition, DO, WHILE

IMG

The Implementation Guide: The area in SAP that contains configuration checklists, and in which you can maintain configuration logs. *{Tools {Customizing {Implementation_Guide.*

IMPORT

Compliance

2.2   3.0

Syntax

```
IMPORT f1 [TO g1] f2 [TO g2]... FROM MEMORY [ID
ident].
```

Definition

Retrieves from user-assigned memory the values of data objects `f1`, `f2,....` The objects can be simple fields, records, table work areas, and internal tables. `f1 TO g1` retrieves the memory data object `f1` into the field `g1`. `ID` selects the objects associated with the label `ident`.

System variables

SY-SUBRC	Description
0	Successful
>0	Otherwise

Cross-reference

See also `EXPORT`

INCLUDE

Compliance

Syntax

```
INCLUDE progname.
```

Definition

Includes the code in the external program `progname` in the current program for syntax tests and operation. The entire `INCLUDE` statement must appear alone on one line. The location of the INCLUDE statement in your program depends on its contents: If it contains DATA statements, it should be located where the program's DATA statements are normally located; if it contains FORMs, then it should be located where the programs FORMs should be (that is, at the end). You can nest INCLUDE programs, that is, one INCLUDE can call another. Program RSINCL00 can create a list of INCLUDE programs and expand their code.

INCLUDE STRUCTURE struct

See DATA

Indirect addressing

See ASSIGN, PERFORM

INFOTYPES

Compliance

Syntax

INFOTYPES nnnn

[NAME name1] "name of the structure

[OCCURS nocc1] "replicate it nocc1 times

[MODE N] "using Logical Databases PNP and PCH—see online help

[VALID FROM date1 TO date2] . "using Logical Database PNP within the date range

Definition

An infotype is a structure in the data dictionary (a table structure containing no data) that is used by the Human Resources module. This command establishes a link to the named data dictionary object and declares an `itab` with the structure of that object. If the HR module is in use, use `SHOW INFOTYPES` in the ABAP/4 Editor to see the list of types; and `SHOW INFOTYPES nnnn` to see details about that specific structure.

Example

```
DATA BEGIN OF name1 OCCURS nocc1.

    INCLUDE STRUCTURE Pnnnn.

DATA END OF name1 VALID BETWEEN date1 AND date2.
```

Table 1.3   Infotype Categories

nnnn	Type of Structure
0000—0999	Master data types
1000—1999	Planning data types
2000—2999	Time tracking data types
3000—8999	(Unused to date)
9000—9999	Customer-defined data types

Initial Values

Variable TYPE	Initial Value
C	(Filled with spaces)
N	(Filled with zeros)
D	'00000000'

Initial Values

Variable TYPE	Initial Value
T	'000000'
I	0
P	0
F	0.0E+00
X	(Filled with zeros, two per byte)

INITIALIZATION

Compliance

2.2   3.0

Syntax

INITIALIZATION.

Definition

Event triggered one time by the selection screen of the program or its Logical Database before the selection is displayed. You can set the PARAMETERS and SELECT-OPTIONS defaults at this point.

Cross-reference

See also "Events" for their triggering order.

INSERT dbtab

Compliance

2.2   3.0

Syntax

```
INSERT dbtab [FROM wa].
```

Definition

Inserts a new record from the header line into `dbtab`. `FROM wa` inserts a new record from work area `wa`, following the structure of `dbtab`. `wa` must be at least as wide as `dbtab`. Duplicate keys and existing `UNIQUE` indexes are not inserted.

System variables

SY-SUBRC	Description
0	The record was inserted
>0	Key violation
SY-DBCNT	Contains the number of records inserted (0 or 1)

Cross-reference

See also `DELETE`, `MODIFY`, `UPDATE`

INSERT dbtab FROM TABLE

Compliance

| 2.2 | | 3.0 | for the main command |

| 3.0 | for options marked with [3.0] |

Syntax

```
INSERT dbtab FROM TABLE itab

    [ACCEPTING DUPLICATE KEYS [3.0]].
```

INSERT dbtab FROM TABLE

Definition

Inserts all the records from internal table `itab`, following the structure of `dbtab`. `itab` must be at least as wide as `dbtab`. Key violations produce runtime errors; `ACCEPTING DUPLICATE KEYS` skips over key violations without producing runtime errors; the remaining records in `itab` are inserted and SY-SUBRC is set to 4.

System variables

SY-SUBRC	Description
0	All requested records were inserted or if `itab` is empty
4	Key violation and `ACCEPTING DUPLICATE KEYS` is chosen
SY-DBCNT	Contains the number of records inserted

Cross-reference

See also `DELETE, MODIFY, UPDATE`

INSERT INTO dbtab

Compliance

Syntax

`INSERT INTO dbtab VALUES wa.`

Definition

Equivalent to `INSERT dbtab [FROM wa].`

INSERT ... INTO fg

Compliance

| 2.2 | 3.0 |

Syntax

```
INSERT f1 [f2...] INTO fg.
```

Definition

Defines field group `fg` by inserting the listed field(s) from one or more tables.

Cross-reference

See also CNT(), EXTRACT, FIELD-GROUPS, LOOP, SUM()

INSERT ... INTO itab

Compliance

| 2.2 | | 3.0 | for the main command

| 3.0 | for options marked with [3.0]

Syntax

```
INSERT

[ INITIAL LINE [3.0]

| LINES OF itab2 [FROM ndx1] [TO ndx2] [3.0]

| wa ] [3.0]

INTO itab1

[INDEX ndx].
```

Definition

Inserts a new record from the header line into itab. INITIAL LINE inserts a new record with all fields initialized. LINES OF itab2 inserts all the records in itab2. FROM ndx1 starts inserting from record number ndx1 of itab2 where ndx1 > 0. TO ndx2 inserts down to and including record number ndx2 of itab2 where ndx2 >= ndx1. wa inserts the new record from work area wa. INDEX ndx inserts the new record into record number ndx, pushing the former record ndx to position ndx+1.

System variables

SY-SUBRC	Description
0	The INDEX option was not used and the record was inserted
4	The index was too large

Cross-reference

See also DELETE, MODIFY, UPDATE

INSERT REPORT

Compliance

Syntax

INSERT REPORT rpt1 FROM itab.

Definition

Inserts into the library the source code of program rpt1. itab must be no wider than 72 characters.

System variables

SY-SUBRC	Description
0	The program was deleted
>0	Otherwise

Cross-reference

See also INSERT TEXTPOOL, DELETE REPORT, READ REPORT

INSERT TEXTPOOL

Compliance

Syntax

INSERT TEXTPOOL rpt1 FROM itab LANGUAGE lng1.

Definition

Assigns the contents of itab to the text elements for program rpt1 in language lng1 and adds them to the library. See READ TEXTPOOL for the structure of itab. Use the system variable SY-LANGU for lng1 to get the language selected at login.

System variables

SY-SUBRC	Description
0	The textpool was read
>0	Otherwise

Cross-reference

See also `DELETE TEXTPOOL`, `READ TEXTPOOL`, Text elements

instance

Definition

There are three types of instances in a SAP system. The application server instance, consisting of a dispatcher and all its work processes, the Message server, and Gateway server. A typical system has a Message server, a Gateway server, and some number of Application servers.

Cross-reference

See also Dispatcher, SAPSYSTEM, Work processes

INT(x)

The "integer" function uses `TRUNC ( x )`.

interactive report

Definition

Event-driven views of lists (reports) with drill-down capability to detailed lists. The Help documentation states that interactive reports are limited to nine levels of drill-down, however, properly written programs seem to just keep going well beyond nine levels without a problem. The events involved in lists are `START-OF-SELECTION`, `GET...`, `END-OF-SELECTION`, `TOP-OF-PAGE...`, `AT PFnn`, `AT LINE-SELECTION`, `AT USER-COMMAND`. To return to the next higher level the user can press the "Back" (F3) function. To return to any higher level in code, the user assigns to SY-LSIND the level's value. The cursor line string is in SY-LISEL upon valid selection. `HIDE` key field data to determine which record was selected.

System variables

Table 1.4   System Fields of Interest to Interactive Reporting

Field	Description
List information	
SY-TITLE	Report title from text elements or attributes
SY-LINCT	Number of lines in the list
SY-LINSZ	Line width in the list
SY-PAGNO	Current page number in the list
SY-LINNO	Current line number in the list
SY-COLNO	Current column number in the list
Window information	
SY-SROWS	Number of lines in the window
SY-SCOLS	Number of columns in the window
SY-CUROW	Current row in the window
SY-CUCOL	Current column in the window
SY-CPAGE	Current page in the window
SY-STARO	Window top displacement in rows
SY-STACO	Window left displacement in columns
Line information	
SY-LSIND	Detail level currently being generated; base list = 0
SY-LISTI	Detail level selected
SY-LILLI	Line number of selected line in window
SY-LISEL	Contents of selected line

Interrupt

There is no interrupt facility available to programmers in SAP except for the events. Those events may be triggered externally by using the "C" program SAPEVT; see the CD, "R/3 System Online Documentation" for information, following the path:

BC Basis

ABAP/4 Development Workbench

BC Basis Programming interfaces

Programming with the Background Processing System

Programming Techniques

Using Events to Trigger Job Starts

Triggering Events from External Programs

IS INITIAL

Definition

SAP relational condition: True when the object of this clause equals its initial value. It may be used in `CHECK`, `ELSEIF`, `IF`, `WHILE`; it may **not** be used in `WHERE`.

Cross-reference

See also Initial Values

itab

Definition

An internal (runtime) table that may contain query results, selection ranges, or working data. Each `itab` has an `INDEX`, which is a unique record number used by several commands. The "standard key" for an `itab` is the concatenation of all its fields that are not numeric (F, I, P) and not internal tables themselves; the standard key doesn't necessarily specify unique records. The commands and system fields that affect `itabs` include: `APPEND, CLEAR, COLLECT, DELETE, DESCRIBE, EDITOR CALL, FREE, INSERT, LOOP, MODIFY, PROVIDE, READ, REFRESH, SEARCH, SELECT, SORT, SPLIT, SUM, UPDATE, SY-TFILL, SY-TLENG, SY-TMAXL, SY-TNAME, SY-TOCCU, SY-TPAGI, SY-TTABC, SY-TTABI`.

Cross-reference

See also Header Line

Language

See `SET LANGUAGE`.

Launch a program

Launch another ABAP/4 program or report

See `SUBMIT`

Launch an operating system (that is, UNIX or Windows NT) program on the application server

See `OPEN DATASET...FILTER`

LDB

See Logical Database

LE

Relational operator "Less than or Equal"—see Operators

LEAVE

Compliance

| 2.2 | | 3.0 | for the main command |

| 3.0 | for options marked with [3.0] |

Syntax

```
LEAVE

[PROGRAM [3.0]] .
```

Definition

Forces an immediate return to the calling program from a report called
with SUBMIT...AND RETURN or a transaction called with CALL
TRANSACTION or CALL DIALOG. LEAVE has no effect in a report
called by SUBMIT or a transaction called with LEAVE TO TRANSAC-
TION or with a transaction code in the command field. The IMPORT
objects are returned from the CALL DIALOG.

LEAVE PROGRAM is identical to LEAVE except that it forces a return to
the transaction selection screen from a report called by SUBMIT or a
transaction called with LEAVE TO TRANSACTION or with a transaction code in the command field.

Cross-reference

See also CHECK, CONTINUE, EXIT, REJECT, STOP

LEAVE LIST PROCESSING

Compliance

| 3.0 |

Syntax

```
LEAVE LIST PROCESSING.
```

Definition

Forces a return to the online transaction from the list-processing mode initiated by LEAVE TO LIST PROCESSING. Processing continues with the PBO of the return screen. If the operator will interactively return to the online transaction with *F3* (Back) or *F15* (Exit), then use of this command is unnecessary.

LEAVE [TO] SCREEN

Compliance

2.2 **3.0** for the main command

3.0 for options marked with [3.0]

Syntax

```
LEAVE {SCREEN

| TO SCREEN scr [3.0] }.
```

Definition

Moves to the next default screen or to screen scr to continue processing in an online transaction. If scr = 0 then processing continues after the calling CALL SCREEN command.

Cross-reference

See also SET SCREEN

LEAVE TO LIST PROCESSING

Compliance

| 2.2 | 3.0 |

Syntax

```
LEAVE TO LIST PROCESSING [AND RETURN TO SCREEN
scr].
```

Definition

Branches from the online transaction to the list-processing mode. The list-processing mode completes with LEAVE LIST PROCESSING or with the operator selecting *F3* (Back) or *F15* (Exit). Upon return, processing continues with the PBO of the screen that controls the list, or optionally of screen scr.

LEAVE TO TRANSACTION

Compliance

| 2.2 | 3.0 |

Syntax

```
LEAVE TO TRANSACTION tcode [AND SKIP FIRST SCREEN].
```

Definition

Flushes all nested or stacked transaction calls, then calls transaction tcode. At completion, processing will continue with the original calling program. AND SKIP FIRST SCREEN will attempt to process the first screen in the background using SAP/GPA memory objects previously defined as PIDs or with SET PARAMETER. Since SY-TCODE contains the name of the current transaction, you can flush the stack of calls and re-start it with LEAVE TO TRANSACTION SY-TCODE.

Cross-reference

See also CALL TRANSACTION

Line-break

See *NEW-LINE*

LOCAL

Compliance

| 2.2 | 3.0 |

Syntax

LOCAL {f | <fs>}.

Definition

Use in a FORM...ENDFORM subroutine to limit the scope of global field f or field-symbol <fs> to the current subroutine. The subroutine picks up the global value and attributes of the field or field-symbol. Upon return from the subroutine, the values of the field or field-symbol are restored to their values before the subroutine is called.

Cross-reference

See also CONSTANTS, DATA, STATICS, TABLES, TYPES

LOG

Compliance

| 2.2 | 3.0 |

Syntax

```
LOG( y ).
```

Definition

Logarithm base *e* of floating-point number y, for $y > 0$.

Cross-reference

See also Arithmetic functions

LOG10

Compliance

3.0

Syntax

```
LOG10( y ).
```

Definition

Logarithm base 10 of floating-point number y, for $y > 0$.

Cross-reference

See also Arithmetic functions

Logical Database

A pre-defined hierarchical structure of database tables, linked with foreign keys for reporting purposes, and an associated ABAP/4 program that reads all their records in hierarchical order. You can create and display Logical Databases in transactions */SLDB*[=i] and */SE36*.

See Part X GET, REPORT

Logical Expressions

See Condition, Operators

LOOP ... ENDLOOP

Compliance

2.2   3.0

Syntax

```
LOOP ... ENDLOOP.
```

Definition

Processes the current data set of extracted field groups.

Cross-reference

See also CNT(), EXTRACT, FIELD-GROUPS, INSERT, ON CHANGE OF, SUM

LOOP AT itab

Compliance

2.2   3.0   for the main command

3.0   for options marked with [3.0]

Syntax

```
LOOP AT itab
```

```
[ INTO wa [3.0]

| TRANSPORTING NO FIELDS] [3.0]

[FROM ndx1] [3.0]

[TO ndx2] [3.0]

[WHERE condition].

. . .

ENDLOOP.
```

Definition

Loops through `itab` and fills the header line (or optionally, work area `wa`) with the contents of the current record. If `itab` has no header line, then you must loop `INTO wa`. `TRANSPORTING NO FIELDS` doesn't fill the header line or `wa`; use this option to count the number of found records. `FROM ndx1` starts looping from record number `ndx1` where `ndx1 > 0`. `TO ndx2` loops down to and including record number `ndx2` where `ndx2 >= ndx1`. The comparisons in `condition` must start with a subfield in the structure of `itab`.

`CONTINUE` unconditionally jumps to `ENDLOOP` for the next iteration. `CHECK <condition>` skips to `ENDLOOP` for the next iteration if the condition is false, and continues execution with the next command if it's true. `EXIT` immediately terminates the loop.

The following conditions are available in loops if the `FROM`, `TO`, or `WHERE` options are **not** used:

Condition	True...
AT FIRST	During the first iteration
AT NEW f1	When f1 (or one of the fields to its left) has just changed
AT END OF f1	When f1 (or one of the fields to its left) will change at the next record
AT LAST	During the last iteration

System variables

SY-SUBRC	Description
0	After ENDLOOP if any records were found
>0	Otherwise
SY-TABIX	Current record number while in the loop; returns to its original value after ENDLOOP
SY-TFILL	Current number of records in itab inside the loop and after ENDLOOP
SY-TOCCU	The declared OCCURS value for itab inside the loop and after ENDLOOP

Cross-reference

See also APPEND, AT...ENDAT, COLLECT, DELETE, DO, INSERT, MODIFY, READ TABLE, SORT, WHILE

LOOP AT SCREEN

Compliance

2.2   3.0

Syntax

```
LOOP AT SCREEN.   ... ENDLOOP.
```

Definition

While in a screen, the system itab SCREEN contains the following attributes of all the fields in the screen. LOOP AT SCREEN provides the ability to alter those attributes at runtime in the PBO module.

LOOP AT SCREEN

Table 1.5   The Structure of *SCREEN*

Field Name	Length	TYPE	Description
Screen-Name	30	C	Field name
Screen-Group1	3	C	Identifies field group 1
Screen-Group2	3	C	Identifies field group 2
Screen-Group3	3	C	Identifies field group 3
Screen-Group4	3	C	Identifies field group 4
Screen-Required	1	C	[1] mandatory input
Screen-Input	1	C	[1] field can accept input
Screen-Output	1	C	[1] field will be displayed
Screen-Intensified	1	C	[1] highlighted field
Screen-Invisible	1	C	[1] invisible field
Screen-Length	1	X	Field length
Screen-Active	1	C	[2] active

Notes:

[1] value = 1 to set the attribute, = 0 to clear it

[2] Screen-Active = 0 is equivalent to Input = 0, Output = 0, and Invisible = 1

Lower case

See TRANSLATE

LT

Relational operator "Less Than"—see Operators.

macros

See DEFINE

MESSAGE

Compliance

2.2   3.0

Syntax

```
MESSAGE {tnnn[(msgid)] | ID msgid TYPE t NUMBER
nnn}

[WITH f1 [f2 [f3[ f4]]]]

[RAISING exception1].
```

Definition

Sends message number nnn from the message-id group specified or shown in the REPORT statement. WITH f1... inserts up to four parameters (up to 50 characters each) in the message consecutively at the positions of the and characters in the message text. RAISING exception1—within a function module, triggers the exception.

The text of messages is stored in table T100;

After a MESSAGE command completes, the seven system fields shown below are assigned; use the following syntax to issue the online message returned from CALL TRANSACTION:

```
MESSAGE ID SY-MSGID TYPE SY-MSGTY NUMBER SY-MSGNO
   WITH SY-MSGV1 SY-MSGV2 SY-MSGV3 SY-MSGV4.
```

Table 1.6	The Message Types *t*	
Type	**Name**	**Description**
A	abend (abnormal end)	Operator must restart transaction
E	error	Operator must enter new correct data
I	information	Operator must press Enter to continue
S	success	Notification on following screen
W	warning	Operator must enter new correct data or press Enter
X	exit	The transaction was terminated with a short dump

Message server—an instance of the SAP system

Cross-reference

See also Gateway server, Instance

MOD

Arithmetic modulo operator (remainder from integer division), see Operators.

MODIFY dbtab

Compliance

2.2 **3.0**

Syntax

```
MODIFY dbtab....
```

Definition

Executes UPDATE if the key is already present in dbtab, and executes INSERT otherwise. MODIFY is expensive; use UPDATE or INSERT if you can determine which applies. The syntax is identical to that of UPDATE and INSERT.

MODIFY itab

Compliance

2.2 **3.0** for the main command

3.0 for options marked with [3.0]

Syntax

```
MODIFY itab

[FROM wa] [3.0]

[INDEX ndx].
```

Definition

Overwrites the current record of itab from the header line or optionally from work area wa. INDEX ndx overwrites record ndx of itab; if record ndx is not present in itab, then no action takes place.

System variables

SY-SUBRC	Description
0	Successful
>0	Otherwise

Cross-reference

See also APPEND and INSERT

MODIFY ... LINE

Compliance

Syntax

```
MODIFY { CURRENT LINE | LINE n1 [OF CURRENT PAGE |
OF PAGE p1 | INDEX ndx] }

    [ FIELD VALUE f1 [FROM g1] [f2 [FROM g2...] ] ]

    [ FIELD FORMAT f1 f_format1 [f2 f_format2...] ]

    [ LINE FORMAT l_format3 ] .
```

Definition

The CURRENT LINE option modifies the current line on the list, then writes the revised string back to the line. The LINE n1 option modifies, line n1. The OF CURRENT PAGE option modifies the selected line on the current page (the default). OF PAGE p modifies the selected line on page p of the list. INDEX ndx modifies the selected line on the list level identified by that index. List value f1 is changed to the value of the variable f1 or g1. Field and line attributes are set by f_format and l_format, which are described in FORMAT.

System variables

SY-SUBRC	Description
0	The line exists
>0	Otherwise
SY-LISEL	Contains the last-read line that is modified
SY-LISTI	Contains the index of the of the last read
SY-LILLI	Contains the line number last read
SY-CPAGE	Contains the page number of the last read
SY-LSIND	Contains the index of the current screen

MODULE

Compliance

Syntax

```
MODULE mod1

[ ON [CHAIN] INPUT

| ON [CHAIN] REQUEST

| AT EXIT-COMMAND

| AT CURSOR-SELECTION].
```

Definition

In Screen Painter flow control, calls module mod1 located in the associated module pool. ON INPUT calls the module only if the triggering field has a non-initial value. ON REQUEST calls the module only if the triggering field has a new value. ON CHAIN INPUT calls the module only if any field in the chain has a non-initial value. ON CHAIN RE-QUEST calls the module only if any field in the chain has a new value. AT EXIT-COMMAND calls the module before the input checks if the screen triggered a type E function. AT CURSOR-SELECTION calls the module if the screen triggered a type S function CS (typically F2).

Cross-reference

See also Flow Control, LEAVE [TO] LIST PROCESSING

MODULE ... ENDMODULE

Compliance

2.2	3.0

Syntax

```
MODULE mod1 {OUTPUT | [INPUT]}. ... ENDMODULE.
```

Definition

A code block in a module pool containing ABAP/4 code that handles online processing events from Screen Painter flow control. OUTPUT specifies a module that will called from a PBO. INPUT specifies a module that will be called from a PAI; this is the default so it can be left off.

MOVE

Compliance

| 2.2 | 3.0 | for the main command |

| 3.0 | for the variation marked with [3.0] |

Syntax

```
MOVE a[+p1(w1)] TO b[+p2(w2)].[PERCENTAGE n
[RIGHT]].
```

or

```
MOVE a[+p3(w3)] TO b[+p4(w4)]. [3.0]
```

Definition

Assignment, equivalent to `b+pn(wn)` = `a+pm(wm)`. The offsets and widths must be literals in Release 2.2, and they may be mixed literals and variables in Release 3.0. Unlike fields are converted; see "Type Conversions" for conversion information.

Example

```
p1 = 5.   w1 = 3.
p2 = 2.   w2 = 1.
s1 = '1234567890'.
S2 = 'ABCDEFGHIJ'.
MOVE s2+2(1) TO s1+5(3). → s1 contains '12345C
90' [2.2]
MOVE s2+p2(W2) TO s1+p1(W1). → s1 contains '12345C
90' [3.0]
```

`PERCENTAGE n`

Transfers the left-most n percent of the **declared** length of `source` to `target`, and left-justifies it in `target` unless `RIGHT` is specified. `a` and `b` must be TYPE C fields; n is a field with a numeric value between 0 and 100. If n < 0, the command will use 0, if n > 100, it will use 100. Use this for displaying "progress thermometers," etc.

Example

```
DATA: cvar1(100), cvar2(50), cpct(3).
PARAMETERS: percent(4) TYPE I DEFAULT 25.
cpct = percent.
cpct+2 = '%'.
cvar1 =
'....1....2....3....4....5....6....7....8....9....0'.
MOVE cvar1 TO cvar2 PERCENTAGE percent.
WRITE: / cpct, cvar2. →    25%
....1....2....3....4....5
```

Note that it assigned 25 percent of the declared length (100), not of the actual length (50).

Cross-reference

See also =, `MOVE-CORRESPONDING`, `WRITE TO`

MOVE-CORRESPONDING

Compliance

Syntax

```
MOVE-CORRESPONDING array1 TO array2.
```

Definition

If `array1` and `array2` are structured work areas such as header lines, then this command assigns values between **like-named** fields of `array1` and `array2`. It is equivalent to:

```
MOVE array1-key1 TO array2-key1.
MOVE array1-key2 TO array2-key2.
...
```

MULTIPLY

Compliance

Syntax

```
MULTIPLY a BY b.
```

Definition

Equivalent to `a = a * b`. Non-numeric fields are converted, see Part VIII for conversion information.

Cross-reference

See also ADD, `DIVIDE`, `SUBTRACT`

MULTIPLY-CORRESPONDING

Compliance

Syntax

```
MULTIPLY-CORRESPONDING array1 TO array2.
```

Definition

If `array1` and `array2` are structured work areas such as header lines, then this command multiplies **like-named** fields in `array1` and `array2`. It is equivalent to:

```
MULTIPLY array1-key1 BY array2-key1.
MULTIPLY array1-key2 BY array2-key2.
. . .
```

Cross-reference

See also ADD-CORRESPONDING, DIVIDE-CORRESPONDING, SUBTRACT-CORRESPONDING

Names

Definition

Field names are limited to 30 characters and must include at least one non-number character; they may not include spaces, parentheses, pluses, minuses, hyphens, commas, or periods. Reserved words may not be used for field names: ABAP/4 keywords are all reserved; INITIAL and SPACE are reserved words; all the words that appear as options ("additions") in commands should be considered reserved, such as EXPORTING, CHANGING, INDEX, etc.

Names

Program names are limited to eight characters that may be letters, numbers, and the underscore. SAP requires that the name for a user-created program must begin with "Y" or "Z". They suggest you assign the letters as follows.

Table 1.7   Program Name Construction

Letter	Description
First Letter—Indicates a User Program	
Y	Will remain in development environment
Z	Will be transported to test and production environments
Second Letter—Indicates the SAP Application	
A	AM—Assets Management
C	PP—Production Planning
E	EDI
F	FI—Financial Accounting
G	GL—General Ledger
I	PM—Plant Management
K	CO—Controlling
M	MM—Materials Management
P	PS—Project System
Q	QM—Quality Management
R	EIS—Executive Information System
S	Basis
U	Utility
V	SD—Sales and Distribution
Y	System

Letter	Description
Third Letter—Indicates the Type of Program	
F	Function programs
I	Include module
P	Report programs
V	Update report
N	Include module
I	Input interface program (that is, BDC input)
O	Output interface
Letters four through seven	
	Any 4-character acronym that may have meaning to the program
Eighth Letter	
	Leave it empty so it's available for future revisions or other options

Names of other objects vary in length and construction. SAP requires that the name for many user-created objects must begin with "Z" or "Z_" if you intend to move the object to production.

NB

Relational operator "Not Between"—see Operators

NE

Relational operator "Not Equal"—see Operators

NEW-LINE

Compliance

2.2 3.0

Syntax

```
NEW-LINE [[NO] SCROLLING].
```

Definition

Creates a new line in a report. This is ignored if the current line is empty (it won't skip blank lines). NO SCROLLING locks subsequent lines from horizontal scrolling, creating title lines. SCROLLING clears the horizontal scroll lock (default).

NEW-PAGE

Compliance

2.2 3.0

Syntax

```
NEW-PAGE
```

[NO-TITLE] "ceases printing title, date and page number (default on detail lists)

[WITH-TITLE] "starts printing title, data and page number (default for basic lists)

[NO-HEADING] "ceases printing column headings (default on detail lists)

[WITH-HEADING] "starts printing column headings (default on basic lists)

[LINE-COUNT lin] "sets new number of lines per page

[LINE-SIZE col]. "sets new number of columns per line

Definition

Starts a new page in a report. This is ignored if the current page is empty (it won't create blank pages). It triggers the TOP-OF-PAGE event but **not** the END-OF-PAGE event. LINE-COUNT sets new number of lines per page; lin = 0 for unlimited length; the default is the value in REPORT LINE-COUNT. LINE-SIZE sets new number of columns per line; col = 0 for standard window width and is effective only at the top of a list level, that is, before the first WRITE or SKIP; the default is the value in REPORT LINE-SIZE.

System variables

SY-LSIND contains the current page number.

NP

String comparison operator "Not contains Pattern"—see Operators.

Notation, York-Mills

See Part XII

Object Linking and Embedding

see OLE

Object names

See Names

OKCODES

Definition

In screen processing, the name of an event triggered by the user or issued in SET USER-COMMAND; and in BDC sessions, the name of an event trigger forced by the session.

The following is a description of the "Use" column:

[1] Some commands are trapped and processed by R/3, so they aren't available in list processing.

[2] User commands defined in the Menu Painter are available in SY-UCOMM for processing in AT USER-COMMAND and AT LINE-SELECTION.

[3] Most OKCODES can be used in BDC sessions.

Table 1.8   List of Some OKCODES

OKCODE	Use	Description
/nn	[3]	Function Key nn
/0 (zero)	[3]	Enter (This works but there is no documentation for it)
/8	[3]	F8; Continue or Execute
/11	[3]	F11; Post
%EX	[1][2]	Exit—Depart this process (yellow up arrow)
%SC	[1]	Display the dialog box "Find by…"
BACK	[1][3]	F3; Return to previous screen, ignoring required entries (same as EXIT)
CS	[1][3]	F2; Select; double-click; (replaces PICK)
DLT	[1][2][3]	F14; Delete
EXIT	[1][3]	F15; Return to previous screen, ignoring required entries (same as BACK)
FCnn	[2]	"Function Key" nn created by SELEC-TION-SCREEN... FUNCTION KEY

OKCODE	Use	Description
HELP	[2]	*F1*; Show the help screen for the current field
LIST	[2] [3]	*F4*; List the possible entries for the current field
MENU	[2] [3]	*F10*; Move focus to the menu
P- -	[1] [3]	*F21*; Scroll up to top of list (use SCROLL in screen processing)
P-	[1] [3]	*F22*; Scroll page up
P+	[1] [3]	*F23*; Scroll page down
P++	[1] [3]	*F24*; Scroll down to end of list
PFnn	[2]	Function Key nn
PICK	[1] [3]	*F2*; Select; double-click; (replaced by *CS*)
PRI	[1] [3]	*F13*; Print
RW	[1] [3]	*F12*; Cancel (that is, Rollback Work)
SAVE	[2] [3]	*F11*; Save
tcode	[3]	Call transaction *tcode*

Cross-reference

See also Part VII, AT USER-COMMAND, AT LINE-SELECTION, SET USER-COMMAND

OLE (Object Linking and Embedding)

Definition

The Microsoft protocol for connecting data between applications; see the OLE commands: CALL METHOD, CREATE OBJECT, FREE OBJECT, GET PROPERTY, SET PROPERTY.

ON CHANGE OF

Compliance

2.2 3.0

Syntax

```
ON CHANGE OF f1 [OR f2 [OR f5...]].  ... ENDON.
```

Definition

Control block used in GET events and SELECT...ENDSELECT loops that is executed in the first record and whenever any of the listed fields change. It is not executed in the last record unless its value just changed.

Cross-reference

See also AT END OF..., AT NEW...

OPEN CURSOR

Compliance

2.2 3.0

Syntax

```
OPEN CURSOR cname FOR SELECT (select parameters).
```

Definition

Creates table cursor cname in the table generated by the SELECT command and initially locates it in the first record of that table. Any SELECT command can be used that produces a table (that is, SELECT SINGLE and aggregates are not allowed). Records in that resultant table can be read with FETCH. cname must be TYPE CURSOR.

Table cursors are closed by screen changes, CLOSE CURSOR, COMMIT WORK, RFCs, and ROLLBACK WORK.

Cross-reference

See also FETCH, CLOSE CURSOR

OPEN DATASET

Compliance

| 2.2 | 3.0 |

Syntax

OPEN DATASET filename FOR {INPUT | OUTPUT | APPENDING}

IN {BINARY | TEXT} MODE

[AT POSITION pos] "byte number for the next read or write

[MESSAGE msg] "assigns to msg any operating system message generated by the command, such as "File not found"

[FILTER cmd] "passes the command to the operating system

[TYPE attr]. "passes the attribute string to the operating system

Definition

Opens an external file on the application server. filename must follow operating system conventions (that is, lowercase, forward slashes: '/ tmp/b18'). INPUT is read-only (default). OUTPUT overwrites any existing file. APPENDING writes to the end of any existing file. IN BINARY MODE (default) concatenates subsequent blocks with no delimiter. IN TEXT MODE terminates each block with the new-line character.

NOTE Trailing blanks are truncated when writing in text mode. To create fixed-length records, use binary mode to write each record and append your own line break (CRLF -Hex 0D0A).

FILTER `cmd` passes the input or output file (as appropriate) through the operating system filter `cmd` (for example, UNIX `'compress'` for output files or `'uncompress'` for input files). You can also use this option to launch a UNIX or NT program that is independent of data files. Just use an empty field for `filename`, and send the entire command in `cmd`.

Example

To rename a file in the UNIX operating system:

```
DATA: nullfile,
      unixcmd(80) VALUE 'mv '.
PARAMETERS: ORG_FILENAME(32),
            NEW_FILENAME(32).
unixcmd+4  =  org_filename.
unixcmd+40 = new_filename.
CONDENSE unixcmd.
OPEN DATASET nullfile FILTER unixcmd.
```

READ DATASET attempts to open an unopened file FOR INPUT IN BINARY MODE. TRANSFER attempts to open an unopened file FOR OUTPUT IN BINARY MODE.

Use the debugger to find current file status: /H F3 {Goto {System {System areas <Area = 'Datasets'

System variables

SY-SUBRC	Description
0	Successful
8	Otherwise

Cross-reference

See also CLOSE DATASET, DELETE DATASET, READ DATASET, TRANSFER

Open SQL

Definition

A subset of SQL commands that are executed by R/3 and provide a safety net not available in native SQL. These commands include: CLOSE CURSOR, COMMIT WORK, DELETE, FETCH, INSERT, MODIFY, OPEN CURSOR, ROLLBACK WORK, SELECT, UPDATE.

Cross-reference

See also EXEC SQL

Operators

Compliance

| 2.2 | 3.0 | for the most operators, except |

| 3.0 | for the exponentiation operator marked with [3.0] |

NOTE All operators, including grouping parentheses, must be separated by spaces. For example,

```
x = 1 + ( a + ( b * c ) ).
```

Definition
Arithmetic Operators
See also Arithmetic functions

= (that is, assignment)

+ – * /

** [3.0]

DIV integer division: a DIV b = TRUNC(a / b)

MOD modulo operator (remainder)

Operators

> **NOTE** a MOD b = a—b * (a DIV b)
> where 0 <= (a MOD b) < ABS(b)

Order of precedence for arithmetic operations:

(Evaluated left-to-right, except exponentiation is evaluated right-to-left.)

    grouping operators (parentheses)

    functions

    exponentiation (**)

    DIV MOD * /

    + -

The keyword COMPUTE invokes arithmetic statements; its use is unnecessary.

Bit Operators

Compare two fields, bit-by-bit; b must be one byte wide and can be TYPE C, P, N, or X.

Table 1.9 Bit Operators

Operator	Description
a O b	(One) true if all the '1's in b are also '1's in a
a Z b	(Zero) true if all the '1's in b are '0's in a
a M b	(Mixed) true if, of the '1's in b, at least one bit in a is '0' and at least one is '1'

Boolean Operators

OR   AND   NOT   (there's no XOR in ABAP/4)

Relational Operators

    = or EQ

    >< or <> or NE

    > or GT

    >= or => or GE

    < or LT

    <= or =< or LE

```
BETWEEN v1 AND v2
IN rtab          (rtab is an internal table described in RANGES)
BT               (Between—in rtab only)
NB               (Not Between—in rtab only)
IS INITIAL       (that is, = 0 or ' ' depending on TYPE)
```

Order of precedence for logic operations:

(Evaluated left-to-right until the result is determined, then evaluation stops.)

grouping operators (parentheses)

NOT

AND

OR

Relational Operators

Table 1.10   String Comparison Operators

Operator	Description
a CA b	The string a contains any one or more characters from string b
a NA b	The string a does not contain any characters from string b
a CO b	The string a contains only characters from string b
a CN b	The string a contains any characters not from string b
a CS b	The string a contains the string b (case-insensitive, trailing blanks ignored)
a NS b	The string a does not contain the string b
a CP b	The string a contains the descriptive Pattern b
a NP b	The string a does not contain the descriptive Pattern b

continues

Operators

Table 1.10 Continued	
Pattern Elements in _b_	
Element	**Description**
*	Masks any string
+	Masks any single character
#	Forces the next character to be compared exactly, that is, upper- and lowercase, *, +, #, and trailing spaces

System variables

SY-FDPOS is set to the zero-based offset in a of the first match after each successful string comparison, and to either the length of a or the offset in a of the first mismatch after a failed comparison. For example,

'Que Computer Books' CS 'MP' → SY-FDPOS contains 6

Output length

Definition

The field length as it would be printed in a list (see its Domain definition). For example, TYPE P's output length may be twice its length.

Cross-reference

See also DESCRIBE FIELD

OVERLAY

Compliance

2.2   3.0

Syntax

```
OVERLAY s1 WITH s2 [ONLY s3].
```

Definition

Replaces **spaces** in s1 with the character in that position in s2, leaving s2 unchanged. ONLY s3 replaces the character in s1 with the character in that position in s2 if the s1 character is any one of the characters in the s3, leaving s2 and s3 unchanged.

Example

```
DATA: name(24)  VALUE 'Que Computer Books',
      ul(24)    VALUE '_____',
      date(10)  VALUE '07-04-1997',
      sep(10)   VALUE '//////////'.
OVERLAY name WITH ul. → name contains
'Que_Computer_Books'
OVERLAY date WITH sep ONLY '-.'. → date contains
'07/04/1997'
```

System variables

SY-SUBRC	Description
0	If any character is replaced
>0	Otherwise

Cross-reference

See also the other string-processing commands: CONCATENATE, CONDENSE, REPLACE, SEARCH, SHIFT, SPLIT, STRLEN(), TRANSLATE

Packed field

Definition

A packed field (TYPE P) stores two digits per byte in Binary-Coded Decimal (BCD) format, reserving the first nibble (half-byte) for the sign, so its resolution is one less than twice its length.

Packed field

Cross-reference

See also Type Conversions, Part VIII, UNPACK

page break

See NEW-PAGE

PAI

See PROCESS AFTER INPUT

Parameter ID (PID)

Definition

Label for a default value stored in user's SPA/GPA memory area.

Cross-reference

See GET PARAMETER ID, SET PARAMETER ID

PARAMETERS

Compliance

| 2.2 | 3.0 | for the main command |

| 3.0 | for options marked with [3.0] |

Syntax

PARAMETERS: p1(w1)

[DEFAULT f1]

[TYPE t1 [DECIMALS n] | LIKE v1] "DECIMALS only applies to TYPE P

[LOWER CASE] "allows uppercase and lowercase (that is, for UNIX file names)

[OBLIGATORY] "mandatory entry

[MEMORY ID pid1] "defaults p1 to the value of pid1

[MATCHCODE OBJECT mc1] "assigns matchcode object mc1 to p1

[MODIF ID mid1] "assigns the screen modification group id mid1 to field p1; (see SCREEN-GROUP1 in LOOP AT SCREEN)

[NO DISPLAY] "hides the field; it may be revealed with LOOP AT SCREEN

[AS CHECKBOX], "always TYPE C(1); = 'X' (Yes) or SPACE (No)

[RADIOBUTTON GROUP g1 [DEFAULT 'X']] . [3.0]

Definition

Defines input parameters on a selection screen for a report. Parameter names (that is, p1...) are limited to eight characters in length. The CHECKBOX and RADIOBUTTON 'X' must be capitalized. To use radiobuttons, you must have at least two PARAMETERS commands with the same radiobutton group. When the selection screen opens, the default radiobutton will be "pressed"; if the user presses another, then all other radiobuttons are cleared. Only one radiobutton at a time will be "pressed." The first radiobutton in a group is the default unless you declare a DEFAULT. You must individually test each radiobutton PARAMETERS command in a group; there's no way to test the group.

Cross-reference

See also AT SELECTION-SCREEN, SELECTION-SCREEN, SELECT-OPTIONS

Pattern Characters (Wildcards)

Definition

Table 1.11   Wildcards in SAP Depend on the Environment

Environment	Single Char.	String
Repository Info Sys (SE85)	+	*
String comparisons	+	*
WHERE ... LIKE	_	%
Illegal Password table USR40	?	*
Screen Painter	_	

NOTE   "v" at the beginning or end of the Screen Painter field locates the sign for negative numbers; place a comma or period in the position you want the decimal point.

Pause

ABAP/4 does not include a pause, sleep, or wait command.

PBO

See PROCESS BEFORE OUTPUT

Percentage

See MOVE ... PERCENTAGE

PERFORM

Compliance

 2.2 **3.0**

Syntax

PERFORM formname [(ext_prog_name) | IN PROGRAM
ext_prog_name [IF FOUND]]

TABLES itab1 itab2

USING a1 a2

CHANGING a3. "(the CHANGING attribute must match the
CHANGING VALUE attribute in the called FORM statement)

Definition

Calls a subroutine created by the FORM...ENDFORM statements in the
current report, or in the external report or program ext_prog_name.
Its actual parameters must have matching formal parameters in the de-
fining FORM statement. Parameters are positional; any number of parameters may be included. You can issue multiple calls with the
colon-and-comma construction:

PERFORM formname USING: a11 a12, a21 a22, a31
a32,... .

or

PERFORM formname: USING a11 a12 CHANGING a13 a14,

         USING a21 a22 CHANGING a24, ...

NOTE IN PROGRAM ext_prog_name IF FOUND calls the subroutine in the external program if the subroutine exists, otherwise, it
continues with the next statement. WARNING: IF FOUND is an undocumented option and may not apply to all releases of R/3. IN
PROGRAM (SY-REPID) IF FOUND uses indirect addressing to
call the subroutine in the current program if the subroutine exists,
otherwise, it continues with the next statement.

Pf-status

Definition

In SAP, a "status" or "pf-status" is a transaction screen. Screens are generated in the Screen Painter /SE51, and their menus in the Menu Painter /SE41.

Cross-reference

See also SET PF-STATUS

PID

See Parameter ID

POH

See PROCESS ON HELP-REQUEST

POSITION

Compliance

| 2.2 | 3.0 |

Syntax

POSITION cl.

Definition

The next WRITE statement begins in column cl and overwrites anything previously written from column cl.

Cross-reference

See also WRITE

POV

See PROCESS ON VALUE

Presentation server

Definition

The top layer of SAP's three-layer client-server-server architecture. This is the user's workstation, running the SAPGUI, and is often referred to as the presentation client.

Cross-reference

See also Application server, Database server, SAPGUI

PRINT-CONTROL

Compliance

| 2.2 | 3.0 |

Syntax

```
PRINT-CONTROL
```

[CPI w1]   "characters per inch

[LPI h1]   "lines per inch

[SIZE s1]   "size of typeface

[COLOR]   "color of output

```
{ BLACK | RED | BLUE | GREEN | YELLOW | PINK }]
```

[LEFT MARGIN col1] "left margin in columns

[FONT f1] "name of font

[FUNCTION f2] "sub-argument as found in table TO22D

[LINE lin1] "line number to start this format

[POSITION col2]. "column number to start this format

Definition

Sets the format of subsequent printer output from the current location, or the location specified by either or both of LINE and POSITION. LINE and POSITION may only be used with one or more of the other options. PRINT-CONTROL affects printer output only; use FORMAT to set screen attributes. This command uses the contents of tables TSP03 and TO22D to determine the printer codes required to execute this format; if the format isn't supported by the printer, this command is ignored. TSP03 maps from the Output Device of the assigned printer to its Device Type. TO22D maps from the Device Type and the Print Control to the printer-specific control characters. Those control characters are the escape commands needed to produce the requested format.

Cross-reference

See also FORMAT, WRITE

PROCESS

Compliance

| 2.2 | 3.0 |

Syntax

```
PROCESS {AFTER INPUT | BEFORE OUTPUT | ON HELP-
REQUEST | ON VALUE-REQUEST}.
```

Definition

Events in screen processing, triggered as follows:

AFTER INPUT—The operator pressed a function key or a button, or selected a menu item.

BEFORE OUTPUT—Before the screen is displayed; use this to initialize the field values and attributes.

ON HELP-REQUEST—The operator selected Help (that is, *F1*).

ON VALUE-REQUEST—The operator selected the Possible Entries list (that is, *F4*).

Cross-reference

See also Flow Control

PROGRAM

Compliance

| 2.2 | 3.0 |

Syntax

PROGRAM.

Definition

The header line in module pool source code—equivalent to REPORT.

"Progress Thermometer"

see MOVE ... PERCENTAGE

Property

Definition

An attribute of an OLE object.

Cross-reference

See GET PROPERTY, SET PROPERTY

PROVIDE

Compliance

| 2.2 | 3.0 |

Syntax

```
PROVIDE

  {f1 [f2 ...] | *} FROM itab1

  {g1 [g2 ...] | *} FROM itab2

  [{h1 [h2 ...] | *} FROM itab3 ...]

BETWEEN j1 AND j2.

    ...

ENDPROVIDE.
```

Definition

Loops through itab1, itab2 ... a number of times to retrieve a specific data series. This one is quite tough to describe. For more information, refer to the Online Help.

RAISE

Compliance

2.2   **3.0**

Syntax

`RAISE e1.`

Definition

In a function module, triggers the exception `e1`. If the calling program lists `e1` in the `EXCEPTIONS` list, then processing returns to the caller without assigning `EXPORT` values. Otherwise, the program terminates with an error message.

Cross-reference

See also `MESSAGE...RAISING`

Random number

You can generate pseudo-random numbers in ABAP/4 by using the functions in the function group F052 [3.0]. Use transaction *ISE37 [Function group [Find* to examine the available functions.

RANGES

Compliance

2.2   **3.0**

Syntax

```
RANGES rtab FOR f1.
```

Definition

Creates the internal table `rtab` for the field `f1`, which the program can then populate with conditions to be used in an `IN` condition. Multiple records are interpreted as `OR` alternatives. Supported relational operators are: `EQ`, `NE`, `GT`, `GE`, `LT`, `LE`, `BT` (BeTween), `NB` (Not Between), `CP` (Contains Pattern), and `NP` (Not contains Pattern). For a pattern (in the Low field) use "+" for single characters and "*" for any number of characters. A range table is automatically created by `SELECT-OPTIONS`. The condition `IN rtab` may be used in `CHECK`, `IF`, `SELECT`, `SUBMIT`, `WHERE`.

Table 1.12 Structure of the Ranges Table

Field	TYPE	Description
Sign	TYPE C(1)	{I (include) | E (exclude)}
Option	TYPE C(2)	Relational operator
Low	LIKE f1	Comparison value and inclusive low value for BT and NB
High	LIKE f1	Inclusive high value for BT and NB

Cross-reference

See also `SELECT-OPTIONS`

READ DATASET

 2.2   **3.0**

Syntax

```
READ DATASET filename INTO array1 [LENGTH w].
```

Definition

Reads the next record from sequential file `filename` on the application server into the named structure. Attempts to OPEN the unopened file IN BINARY MODE FOR INPUT. IN BINARY MODE reads the number of bytes in `array1`. IN TEXT MODE reads a line (that is, to the next new-line character). LENGTH returns in w the number of characters read. File contents are read literally and without conversion.

System variables

SY-SUBRC	Description
0	Successful
4	End of file
8	Cannot open file

Cross-reference

See also CLOSE DATASET, DELETE DATASET, OPEN DATASET, TRANSFER

READ ... LINE

Compliance

Syntax

```
READ {CURRENT LINE | LINE n

[OF CURRENT PAGE | OF PAGE p]

[INDEX ndx1] }

[FIELD VALUE f1 [INTO g1]].
```

Definition

Reads into SY-LISEL the contents of the current line or of line n of the
current list and refreshes all the hidden values. OF CURRENT PAGE
reads line n on the current page of the list. OF PAGE p reads line n on
page p of the list. INDEX ndx1 reads the line at list level ndx1 (not
appropriate for READ CURRENT LINE). FIELD VALUE f1 assigns
the value of list element f1 (typically an input field, such as a checkbox)
to the variable f1. INTO g1 assigns it into a variable having a different
name. Remember to CLEAR f1 or g1 before each iteration.

System variables

SY-SUBRC	Description
0	A line was read
>0	Otherwise
SY-LISEL	Contains the last-read line, which is modified
SY-LISTI	Contains the index of the of the last read
SY-LILLI	Contains the line number last read
SY-CPAGE	Contains the page number of the last read
SY-LSIND	Contains the index of the current screen

See MODIFY LINE, WRITE

READ REPORT

Compliance

2.2 3.0

Syntax

READ REPORT rpt1 INTO itab.

Definition

Reads program `rpt1` into `itab`; `itab` must be at least 72 characters wide.

System variables

SY-SUBRC	Description
0	The program was read
>0	Otherwise

Cross-reference

See also `DELETE REPORT`, `INSERT REPORT`, `READ TEXTPOOL`

READ TABLE

Compliance

2.2 **3.0** for the main command

3.0 for options marked with [3.0]

Syntax

```
READ TABLE itab [INTO wa]

[INDEX ndx1 | WITH KEY {f1=v1 [f2=v2...] [3.0]
|  k1  |  =k2 [3.0] }

[BINARY SEARCH]]

[COMPARING f1 [f2...] | [ALL FIELDS]]

[TRANSPORTING f1 [f2...] | [NO FIELDS]].
```

Definition

Reads into the header line or work area `wa` the first entry in `itab` whose values match the non-numeric, non-initial fields in the header line or `wa`. `INDEX` reads the entry at record number `ndx1`. `WITH KEY...` reads the first entry:

- whose fields match the variables `v1`, `v2...` (`vn` converted to match `fn`) [3.0],

- whose table line matches the string `k1` (`itab` converted to match `k1`),

- whose table line matches the string `k2` (`k2` converted to match `itab`) [3.0].

You must `SORT` `itab` ascending (by f1, f2... in the case of that `KEY` option) before using `BINARY SEARCH`. `COMPARING...` compares the listed fields or all fields with the header line or `wa` after the line is read. `TRANSPORTING...` assigns just the listed fields or no fields into the header line or `wa`. Use `NO FIELDS` just to set SY-SUBRC and SY-TABIX.

System Variables

Y-SUBRC	Description
0	The read (and the compare if used) succeeded
2	The read succeeded and the compare failed
4	The read failed
SY-TABIX	Record number read if successful

Cross-reference

See also `LOOP...AT`

READ TEXTPOOL

Compliance

| 2.2 | 3.0 |

Syntax

```
READ TEXTPOOL rptl INTO itab LANGUAGE lngl.
```

Definition

Reads from the library into `itab` the text elements for program `rptl` in language `lngl`.

Table 1.13   The Structure of *TEXTPOOL*

Fieldname	Description	Type
ID	ABAP/4 textpool ID (type of text)	C1
Key	Text element key (number or selection name)	C8
Entry	Language-dependent text	C255
Length	Number bytes reserved for the text (with language reserve)	14 [3.0]

Table 1.14   Types of Text in *TEXTPOOL*

Application	ID	Key
Column Heading	H	001-004
Text symbols	I	NNN
Report or Program titles	R	(blank)
List Headings	T	(blank)
Selection Texts	S	Name up to 8 Characters

System variables

SY-SUBRC	Description
0	The textpool was read
>0	Otherwise

Cross-reference

See also `DELETE TEXTPOOL`, `INSERT TEXTPOOL`, Text elements

RECEIVE RESULTS

Compliance

Syntax

```
RECEIVE RESULTS FROM FUNCTION fnc1

[IMPORTING p1=f1 [p2=f2...]]

[TABLES p1=itab1 [p2=itab2...]]

[EXCEPTIONS e1[=retcode1] [e2[=retcode2...]]].
```

Definition

Receives the results of an asynchronous function (that is, RFC) that was called by using

```
CALL FUNCTION fnc1...
    STARTING NEW TASK taskname
    PERFORMING formname ON END OF TASK.
```

The `RECEIVE RESULTS` command must be in the `FORM` subroutine called by the function calling statement. The parameter list for this `RECEIVE` command must complement that of the function whose results it is receiving, that is, IMPORTING parameters here must match EXPORTING parameters in the function, TABLES must match TABLES in the function, and EXCEPTIONS must match EXCEPTIONS in the function. The FORM subroutine must have a USING taskname parameter in its definition.

System variables

SY-SUBRC	Description
0	No exception raised
n	Exception n was raised
>0	Otherwise

Cross-reference

See also CALL FUNCTION

REFRESH itab

Compliance

Syntax

```
REFRESH itab.
```

Definition

Empties itab; allocated memory is not released; if there is a header line it remains unaffected.

Cross-reference

See also CLEAR, FREE

REFRESH CONTROL

Compliance

| 3.0 |

Syntax

`REFRESH CONTROL ctrl1 FROM SCREEN scr1.`

Definition

Restores `ctrl1` (created by a CONTROLS statement) to its initial value as defined in `scr1`.

See CONTROLS

REJECT

Compliance

| 2.2 | | 3.0 |

Syntax

`REJECT [dbtab].`

Definition

Unconditionally jumps to the bottom of the current GET code block to get the next record of the current table. `dbtab` skips all GET events until the next record of `dbtab` is available. `dbtab` must be at the same or higher hierachical level in the LDB as the current table; it must not be deeper in the hierarchy than the current table.

Cross-reference

See also CHECK, CONTINUE, EXIT, LEAVE, STOP

Relational Operators

See Operators

Remote Function Call (RFC)

Definition

Synchronous or asynchronous call to a function on a system other than that of the caller. The remote system may be another R/3, an R/2, or a C program running on an application server.

Cross-reference

See also CALL FUNCTION and the on-line help

REPLACE

Compliance

Syntax

```
REPLACE string1 [LENGTH w] WITH string2 INTO
string3.
```

Definition

Searches string3 for the first (case-insensitive) occurrence of the first w characters of string1. Removes from string3 those w characters and inserts at that location the contents of string2. string1 and string2 are unchanged.

Example

```
DATA city(20) VALUE 'Austin, TX'.
REPLACE 'TX' WITH 'Texas' INTO city. → city
contains 'Austin, Texas'
```

System variables

SY-SUBRC	Description
0	`string1(w)` was found in `string3`
>0	otherwise

Cross-reference

See also the other string processing commands: CONCATENATE, CONDENSE, OVERLAY, SEARCH, SHIFT, SPLIT, STRLEN(), TRANSLATE

REPORT

Compliance

Syntax

```
REPORT rpt1
```

[LINE-SIZE n] "vs default 80; <= 255

[LINE-COUNT l[(n)]] "l = # lines per page, default 0 (that is, no forced pagination); n = # lines reserved for end-of-page area, default 0

[MESSAGE-ID xx] "online messages from table T100

[NO STANDARD PAGE HEADING]. "suppresses title, date and page no. header

Definition

Defines a report—the first line of the program. The name must have no more than eight characters and not start with "R."

System variables

SY-LINSZ contains the current line-size

SY-LINCT contains the current lines per page

SY-REPID contains the name of the current report

Cross-reference

See also PROGRAM

RESERVE

Compliance

| 2.2 | 3.0 |

Syntax

```
RESERVE n LINES.
```

Definition

In list generation, tests whether more than n lines remain on the page. If not, then it triggers the END-OF-PAGE event, providing that many lines for end-of-page processing. n may be literal or a variable. This command, very hard to get working right, but REPORT rpt1 LINE-COUNT 1(n) works exactly as advertised with no hassle.

Cross-reference

See also BACK

RFC

See Remote Function Call

ROLLBACK WORK

Compliance

 2.2   3.0

Syntax

ROLLBACK WORK.

Definition

Reverses all database changes made since the last COMMIT
WORK. Since this clears all table cursors, don't use it in
SELECT...ENDSELECT loops or with FETCH commands.

Round

See TRUNC, WRITE...ROUND

SAPGUI

Definition

The presentation interface or the "client" in the SAP three-layer client-
server-server architecture; the "top layer" of SAP, above the application
server, residing on the user's terminal.

Cross-reference

See also Application server, Database server, Presentation server

SAPTEMU

Obsolete term for SAPGUI

SAPSYSTEM

Definition

All the instances plus the database make up a system. Available systems are listed in the table TSYST. "System" in SAP is somewhat equivalent to "Instance" in Oracle. Typical systems in an installation are:

Development (or Integration) System

Test (or Quality Assurance or Consolidation) System

Production (or Recipient) System

Cross-reference

See also Instance

SAPSCRIPT

Definition

SAPScript is a means for formatting reports for printed output. See on-line help *[Basis Components [System Administration [Style and Layout Set Maintenance*

screen

See CALL SCREEN, LEAVE SCREEN, Pf-status, SET PF-STATUS, SET SCREEN, SET TITLEBAR

screen attributes table

See LOOP AT SCREEN

SCROLL LIST

Compliance

| 2.2 | 3.0 |

Syntax

```
SCROLL LIST

{ TO FIRST PAGE

| TO LAST PAGE

| TO PAGE p

| FORWARD [n PAGES]

| BACKWARD [n PAGES]

| TO COLUMN c

| LEFT [BY n PLACES]

| RIGHT [BY n PLACES] }

[ LINE r1 ]

[ INDEX ndx1 ].
```

Definition

Scrolls the list in the current list level under program control and high-lights the current line. LINE highlights line r1. INDEX jumps to list level ndx1 then scrolls.

System variables

SY-SUBRC	Description
0	Successful
4	List area exhausted
8	List doesn't exists (that is, index call)
SY-LSIND	Contains the current list level index

SEARCH

Compliance

| 2.2 | 3.0 |

Syntax

```
SEARCH {string1 | itab} FOR string2
```

[ABBREVIATED] "string2 may have missing characters after the first character

[STARTING AT p1] "starting the search at string1 offset p1 or itab record p1

[ENDING AT p2] "ending the search at string1 offset p2 or itab record p2

[AND MARK] . "capitalize the matched substring of string1

Definition

Searches string1 or the table (not the header line) itab for the first case-insensitive delimited substring (that is, word) that matches with the contents of string2. Substring delimiters are SPACE, COMMA,

SEMICOLON, COLON, PERIOD, PLUS, EXCLAMATION POINT, QUESTION MARK, PARENTHESES, FORWARD SLASH, and EQUALS. `string1` and `string2` are treated as character strings without conversion.

Table 1.15 Available Forms of *string2*

Form	Description
`'abc '`	The string `"abc"`, dropping any trailing spaces
`'.abc .'`	The string `"abc"` (including trailing spaces)
`'*abc'`	Any string that ends in `"abc"`
`'abc*'`	Any string that begins with `"abc"`

System variables

SY-SUBRC	Description
0	`string2` was found
>0	Otherwise
SY-FDPOS	(zero-based) Offset of the match in `string1` or in the table line of `itab`
SY-TABIX	Record number in `itab` where the match was found;

Example

```
DATA: s1(24) VALUE 'Que Computer Books'.
SEARCH s1 FOR 'cmptr' ABBREVIATED AND MARK.
WRITE: s1, SY-FDPOS. → Que COMPUTER Books 4
```

Cross-reference

See also the other string-processing commands: CONCATENATE, CONDENSE, OVERLAY, REPLACE, SHIFT, SPLIT, STRLEN(), TRANSLATE

SELECT commands

Compliance

| 2.2 | 3.0 | for the main command

| 3.0 | for options marked with [3.0]

Definition

Retrieves records in random order from a database table or a view, and places in the header line; several forms are illustrated below. The order of the FROM and INTO parameters is not important.

System variables

SY-SUBRC	Description
0	One or more records were retrieved
4	No record was retrieved
8	Key was incomplete (SELECT SINGLE only)
SY-DBCNT	Current number of records retrieved, and the total number after ENDSELECT

Cross-reference

See also Condition, ON CHANGE OF . . .

Syntax

SELECT—basic form

```
SELECT {f1 f2 f3 [3.0] | * } FROM dbtab

   [INTO wa]            "moves the retrieved data into work area wa
```

SELECT commands

    [UP TO n ROWS] "stops selecting when n matching records have been found

    [BYPASSING BUFFER] "gets data directly from the database, not using buffered data

    [WHERE <condition>] "retrieves only records that satisfy the condition

    [ORDER BY {f2 [DESCENDING] [f1 [DESCENDING]...]
| PRIMARY KEY}].

    ...

ENDSELECT.

Definition

Moves selected data from the database table or a view into the corresponding fields of the header line, or optionally into the work area wa. The <condition> may be any simple or compound logical expression on one or more of the field values. Processing of ORDER BY precedes UP TO n ROWS if both options are used. Table cursors are cleared by COMMIT WORK and ROLLBACK WORK so any commands that invoke them shouldn't be used in a SELECT... ENDSELECT loop or before a FETCH command; those commands include CALL SCREEN, CALL TRANSACTION, BREAKPOINT. Using the BYPASSING BUFFER option posts changes directly to the database tables, so subsequent ROLLBACK WORK commands have no effect.

SELECT—columns [3.0]

DATA: w_f1 LIKE dbtab-f1 OCCURS 10, w-f2 LIKE dbtab-f2 OCCURS 10.

SELECT [DISTINCT] f1 f2 FROM dbtab

  INTO (w_f1, w_f2)

  [UP TO n ROWS]

    [BYPASSING BUFFER] "unnecessary with DISTINCT

  [WHERE ...]

  [ORDER BY ...].

  ...

ENDSELECT.

Definition

Retrieves selected fields into internal tables. DISTINCT retrieves
unique values of the selected fields. The data are available after
ENDSELECT as internal tables.

SELECT—single

```
SELECT SINGLE [FOR UPDATE] {f1 f2 f3... [3.0] | *}
FROM dbtab

    [INTO wa]

    [UP TO n ROWS]

    WHERE key1 = v1 [AND key2 = v2..].
```

Definition

Retrieves the first matching record [3.0], or retrieves the single matching record if the entire key value is specified. No ENDSELECT is
needed. FOR UPDATE protects the selected record from changes by
others until the next COMMIT WORK.

SELECT—Into an Internal Table

```
SELECT

[SINGLE [FOR UPDATE]] [3.0]

{f1 f2 f3... [3.0] | * } FROM dbtab

    {APPENDING | INTO} TABLE itab

    [UP TO n ROWS]

    [BYPASSING BUFFER] "unnecessary with SINGLE

    [WHERE ...]

    [ORDER BY ..].
```

Definition

No ENDSELECT is needed. The SINGLE statement selects the first
matching record. The order of the FROM and APPENDING or INTO
clauses is immaterial.

SELECT—Overall Aggregate

```
DATA: w_cnt TYPE I, w_cntd TYPE I, w_avg LIKE
dbtab-f1...

SELECT AVG( f1 ) [3.0]

  COUNT( f1 )
```

```
        COUNT( DISTINCT f1 ) [3.0]

        MAX( f1 ) [3.0]

        MIN( f1 ) [3.0]

        SUM( f1 ) [3.0]

     FROM dbtab

     INTO (w_avg, w_cnt, w_cntd, w_max, w_min, w_sum)

     [UP TO n ROWS]

        [WHERE ...].
```

Definition
Extracts specified aggregate information (that is, sum, average, etc.) of all the records satisfying the WHERE condition. No ENDSELECT is needed.

SELECT—Grouped Aggregate
DATA: w_cnt TYPE I, w_cntd TYPE I, w_avg LIKE dbtab-f1...

```
SELECT f1 [f2...] [3.0]

  AVG( f1 )

  COUNT( * )

  COUNT( DISTINCT f2 )

....MAX( f1 )

....MIN( f1 )

....SUM( f1 )

....FROM dbtab

....INTO (w_avg, w_cnt, w_cntd, w_max, w_min,
w_sum)

....[UP TO n ROWS]

....[WHERE...]

....GROUP BY f1 [f2...].;these fields must be specified in the
SELECT list

  ...

ENDSELECT
```

Definition

Extracts specified aggregate information (that is, sum, average, etc.) for each combination of the values of the fields listed in the GROUP BY clause, of all the records satisfying the WHERE condition.

SELECT-OPTIONS

Compliance

| 2.2 | 3.0 | for the main command |

| 3.0 | for options marked with [3.0] |

Syntax

```
SELECT-OPTIONS rtab FOR f1
```

[DEFAULT g1 "default "Low" value as described for rtab below

   [TO g2] "default "High" value as described for rtab below

   [OPTION op1] "default "Option" value as described for rtab below

   [SIGN s1]] "default "Sign" value as described for rtab below

[LOWERCASE] "case-insensitive; allows lower and upper case

[MATCHCODE OBJECT mco1] "places the matchcode object in rtab-Low

[MEMORY ID pid1] "places the parameter ID (PID) value in rtab-Low

[MODIF ID mid1] "assigns the screen modification group id mid1 to field f1; (see SCREEN-GROUP1 in LOOP AT SCREEN)

[NO-DISPLAY] "hides the selection from the operator

[NO-EXTENSION] "blocks the 'Multiple Selection' option; allows single entry only

[NO INTERVALS] [3.0] "hides `rtab-High`; allows single values only (that is, no ranges)

[OBLIGATORY]. "entry in `rtab-Low` is mandatory

Definition

Adds selection criteria to the selection screen. This creates for field `f1` an internal table `rtab`, which the user can fill in at the selection screen and with the structure.

Table 1.16 Structure of *itab*

Field	TYPE	Description
Sign	TYPE C(1)	'I' nclude (default) or 'E' xclude
Option	TYPE C(2)	EQ (default), NE, CP, NP, GE, LT, LE, GT, BT, NB
Low	LIKE f1	Comparison value and inclusive low BT | NB value; this field must have the same TYPE as f1
High	LIKE f1	Inclusive high BT | NB value; this field must have the same TYPE as f1

Cross-reference

See also Operators, AT SELECTION-SCREEN, PARAMETERS, RANGES, SELECTION-SCREEN

SELECTION-SCREEN

Compliance

| 2.2 | 3.0 | for the main command |

| 3.0 | for options marked with [3.0] |

Syntax

```
SELECTION-SCREEN

{ {BEGIN | END} OF LINE
```

| BEGIN OF BLOCK b1 [WITH FRAME [TITLE text1]] [NO INTERVALS] [3.0]

| END OF BLOCK b1 [3.0]

| COMMENT [/] p(w) text1 [MODIF ID mid1]

| FUNCTION KEY k [3.0]

| POSITION [p| POS_LOW [3.0] | POS_HIGH [3.0]] [MODIF ID mid1 [3.0]]

| PUSHBUTTON [/] [p] text1 USER-COMMAND cmd1 [MODIF ID mid1] [3.0]

| SKIP n

| ULINE [/] [p| POS_LOW [3.0] | POS_HIGH [3.0]] [(w)] [MODIF ID mid1 [3.0]] }.

Definition

Commands for creating a complex selection screen that the report (program) presents to the user when it begins. text1 takes the form {t1 [3.0]| TEXT-nnn} where t1 is a text variable assigned in the INI-TIALIZATION event and not declared in DATA, and TEXT-nnn is the normal language-specific text element from the text pool. Blocks may be nested up to five deep. WITH FRAME draws a frame around the block on the screen. TITLE places the title text1 in the center of the top line of the frame. NO INTERVALS hides rtab-High on all SELECT-OPTIONS in the block; the NO INTERVALS attribute is inherited in nested blocks WITH FRAME, and not inherited otherwise. / forces a new-line; it is not allowed between BEGIN OF LINE and END OF LINE. n indicates the number of lines to skip, between 1 and 9; blank is equivalent to 1. p and (w) are position and width measured in columns. MODIF ID mid1 assigns the screen modification group id mid1 to the element; (see SCREEN-GROUP1 in LOOP AT SCREEN). FUNCTION KEY n places up to five "function key" pushbuttons in the toolbar at the top of the screen; you must assign their labels in the system table SSCRFIELDS-FUNCTXT_01 through -FUNCTXT_05.

When the operator selects a function key, SY-UCOMM is set to
`'FC01'..'FC05'` as appropriate. `POSITION` must be between
`BEGIN OF LINE` and `END OF LINE`. `POS_LOW` and `POS_HIGH` are
the positions of the Low and High fields created by `SELECT-OPTIONS`.
`cmd1` is the command code assigned to SY-UCOMM when the operator selects the pushbutton, `ULINE (w)` may be used between
`BEGIN OF LINE` and `END OF LINE`; it uses the current position.
`PARAMETERS` and `SELECTION-SCREEN COMMENT` commands may
be placed on `SELECTION-SCREEN` line.

Cross-reference

See also `PARAMETERS, SELECT-OPTIONS`

SET BLANK LINES

Compliance

3.0

Syntax

```
SET BLANK LINES {ON | OFF}.
```

Definition

Allows or suppresses `WRITE`ing of blank lines; `OFF` is the default.

SET COUNTRY c1.

Compliance

3.0

Syntax

```
SET COUNTRY c1.
```

Definition

Sets representation of decimal points and dates in WRITE commands according to the specifications in table T005X. If c1 EQ SPACE then COUNTRY is set to that in the current user's master record.

System variables

SY-SUBRC	Description
0	c1 was found in T005X or c1 EQ SPACE
>0	Otherwise

SET CURSOR

Compliance

2.2   **3.0**

Syntax

```
SET CURSOR

{ FIELD f1 [OFFSET c1] [LINE r1]

| LINE r2 [OFFSET c2]

| c1 r3 }.
```

Definition

Positions the cursor as directed. OFFSET c1 is the zero-based offset in columns from the start of field f1. LINE r1 is required for step-loop (line number) and list processing (SY-LILLI). LINE r2 places the cursor in step loop line or list line (SY-LILLI). OFFSET c2 is the zero-based offset from the start of the line in columns. c1 r3 is the screen position in columns and rows.

Cross-reference

See also GET CURSOR

SET LANGUAGE

Compliance

3.0

Syntax

SET LANGUAGE lng1.

Definition

Sets the language for all text-pool and other language-specific elements; applies only to the current program.

SET LEFT SCROLL-BOUNDARY

Compliance

3.0

Syntax

SET LEFT SCROLL-BOUNDARY [COLUMN c1].

Definition

Sets the left edge of the horizontally scrollable portion of the screen to the current column. COLUMN c1 sets it to column c1. This command applies only to the current screen (set it in the TOP-OF-PAGE event).

SET MARGIN

Compliance

Syntax

SET MARGIN c1[r1].

Definition

Sets the left margin to c1 and the top margin to r1 for lists in the current report.

SET PARAMETER ID

Compliance

2.2   3.0

Syntax

SET PARAMETER ID key FIELD f1.

Definition

Assigns the PID key in the user's SPA/GPA Memory Area to the value of f1.

Cross-reference

See also GET PARAMETER ID

SET PF-STATUS

Compliance

 3.0

Syntax

```
SET PF-STATUS statusID

    [EXCLUDING fnc1 | itab ] [IMMEDIATELY].
```

Definition

Sets the current GUI status (interactive screen) to `statusID`. EXCLUD-ING `fnc1` deactivates function `fnc1`. EXCLUDING `itab` deactivates the functions listed in `itab`, one per record. IMMEDIATELY in list processing forces the new status to take effect at the current list level (in screen processing the new status is set immediately without this option).

System variables

SY-PFKEY contains the identity of the current GUI status.

SET PROPERTY

Compliance

3.0

Syntax

```
SET PROPERTY OF obj1 p1 = f1 [NO FLUSH].
```

Definition

Sets attribute `p1` of the OLE2 object `obj1` to the value of field `f1`. `NO FLUSH` continues OLE2 bundling even if the next statement isn't an OLE2 command.

System variables

SY-SUBRC	Description
0	All OLE2 commands in the bundle were successful
1	Communication error, described in SY-MSGL1
2	Method call error, described in dialog box
3	Property set up error, described in dialog box
4	Property read error, described in dialog box

Cross-reference

See also `CALL METHOD, CREATE OBJECT, FREE OBJECT, GET PROPERTY`

SET SCREEN

Compliance

Syntax

```
SET SCREEN scr1.
```

Definition

Sets the next screen number in an online dialog box. Use `scr1 = 0` to return to the calling `CALL SCREEN`.

SET TITLEBAR

Compliance

Syntax

```
SET TITLEBAR t1 [WITH v1 [v2...]].
```

Definition

Sets the current title bar at the top of the GUI status to `t1`. The contents of `t1` may be up to 70 characters wide. Title bar text is stored and edited in the Menu Painter transaction *ISE41 *Title List*. Up to nine ampersands (and) in the title text will be replaced by parameters `v1`, `v2...` (to show an ampersand in the title, enter two of them, that is, andand).

System variables

SY-TITLE contains the current title bar text.

SET USER-COMMAND

Compliance

Syntax

```
SET USER-COMMAND f1.
```

Definition

In report list generation, when the list is to be displayed, executes the system function code `f1` or `AT USER-COMMAND f1` or `AT LINE-SELECTION`, depending on the contents of `f1`; the system behaves exactly as if the operator had typed f1 into the command field and pressed <Enter> at the current list and cursor positions.

See OKCODES.

SHIFT

Compliance

Syntax

```
SHIFT f1 [RIGHT] [CIRCULAR] [BY n1 PLACES | UP TO
f2].
```

Definition

Shifts strings in a variable; n1 > 0; if n1 > width of f1, then f1 is filled with blanks, except for CIRCULAR. CIRCULAR rotates to the declared width, not the string width. UP TO shifts or rotates until the string in f2 appears at the beginning or end (RIGHT) of f1; if f2 is not found in f1, then no shift takes place.

Example

```
DATA: s1(8) VALUE 'ABCDE_ _ _'.
SHIFT s1. → s1 = 'BCDE_ _ _ _'
SHIFT s1 BY 3 PLACES CIRCULAR. → s1 = 'DE_ _ _ABC'
SHIFT s1 UP TO 'CD' CIRCULAR. → s1 = 'CDE_ _ _AB'
SHIFT s1 RIGHT. → s1 = '_ABCDE_ _'
```

System variables

SY-SUBRC	Description
0	f2 was found (UP TO f2 option only)
>0	f2 was not found (UP TO f2 option only)

Cross-reference

See also the other string processing commands: CONCATENATE,
CONDENSE, OVERLAY, REPLACE, SEARCH, SPLIT, STRLEN(),
TRANSLATE

SHIFT ... DELETING

Compliance

3.0

Syntax

SHIFT f1{LEFT DELETING LEADING | RIGHT DELETING
TRAILING} f2.

Definition

Shifts the string in f1 left or right until the first or last character in f1
matches any of the characters in f2. If no character in f2 appears in
f1, then no shift takes place.

Example

```
DATA: s1(8) VALUE 'ABCDEFGH',
    s2(2) VALUE 'CF'.
SHIFT s1 RIGHT DELETING TRAILING s2. →  s1 =
 '_ _ABCDEF'
SHIFT s1 LEFT DELETING LEADING s2. →  s1 =
'CDEFG_ _'
```

Cross-reference

See also the other string processing commands: CONCATENATE,
CONDENSE, OVERLAY, REPLACE, SEARCH, SPLIT, STRLEN(),
TRANSLATE

SIGN

Compliance

3.0

Syntax

SIGN(x).

Definition

Sign of any number x: $0 \rightarrow 0$; $> 0 \rightarrow 1$; $< 0 \rightarrow -1$.

Cross-reference

See also Arithmetic functions

SIN

Compliance

2.2   3.0

Syntax

SIN(y).

Definition

Sine of floating-point number y, for y in radians.

Cross-reference

See also Arithmetic functions

SINH

Compliance

Syntax

SINH(y).

Definition

Hyperbolic sine of floating-point number y.

Cross-reference

See also Arithmetic functions

SKIP

Compliance

Syntax

SKIP [n1 | TO LINE r1].

Definition

Skips 1 line or n1 lines in a report. SKIP is ignored at the beginning of a page except for the first page of a list and a NEW-PAGE page. If n1 plus the current line number is greater than the LINE-COUNT value less the reserved number of lines, then a new page is started. TO LINE r1 jumps up or down to the (one-based) line number r1 of the report. If r1 is greater than the LINE-COUNT value there's no SKIP.

Cross-reference

See also ULINE, WRITE

Sleep

ABAP/4 does not include a pause, sleep, or wait command.

SORT

Compliance

| 2.2 | 3.0 |

Syntax

```
SORT [DESCENDING] [BY f1 [f2...] | fg1].
```

Definition

Sorts the current extracted dataset ascending (or DESCENDING) by all the fields in the HEADER field-group. BY f1... sorts by the listed fields in the HEADER field-group. BY fg1 sorts by the fields that are in both the HEADER field-group and in field-group fg1.

Cross-reference

See also EXTRACT, FIELD-GROUPS, INSERT, LOOP

SORT itab

Compliance

| 2.2 | 3.0 |

Syntax

```
SORT itab [DESCENDING | BY f1 [DESCENDING]
[f2...]].
```

Definition

Sorts `itab` ascending (or `DESCENDING`) by all non-F,I,P fields. `BY`
`f1`... sorts `itab` by the listed fields (all TYPES are allowed), ascending
except for those fields for which `DESCENDING` is specified.

Cross-reference

See also `APPEND...SORTED BY`

Sound

There's no `BELL`, `BEEP`, or `SOUND` command documented for ABAP/4.

SPA/GPA Memory Area

Definition

The Set Parameter/Get Parameter area in memory set aside to store the
user's PIDs.

See `GET PARAMETER, SET PARAMETER`

SPACE

Definition

ABAP/4 reserved constant = ' ', usable in the constructions:

- X {EQ | NE | <>} SPACE (relation)
- X = SPACE and MOVE SPACE TO X (assignment)

SPLIT

Compliance

Syntax

```
SPLIT s1 AT s2 INTO {tgt1 tgt2 [tgt3...] | TABLE
itab}.
```

Definition

Splits string `s1` at each location of the delimiter `s2` and assigns the substrings in order to the targets `tgt1 tgt2...` or to successive records of `itab`. If there are more substrings than targets, the remainder are all assigned to the last target. If a substring is wider than its target, it is truncated into the target. The full width of the `DATA` declaration of the delimiter is used, regardless of its value. Operands are treated as TYPE C without conversion. Trailing spaces are retained in target assignments, and truncated in `itab` assignments.

Example

```
DATA: delim(2) VALUE ',', t1(6), t2(6), t3(6),
t4(20).
SPLIT 'New Jersey, Texas, California, Ohio, Iowa'
AT delim INTO t1, t2, t3, t4.
→ t1 contains 'New Je'
→ t2 contains 'Texas'
→ t3 contains 'Califo'
→ t4 contains 'Ohio, Iowa'
```

NOTE Notice that the effective delimiter is ', ' because its declared length is 2.

System variables

SY-SUBRC	Description
0	All targets were wide enough
>0	An assignment was truncated

Cross-reference

See also the other string processing commands: CONCATENATE,
CONDENSE, OVERLAY, REPLACE, SEARCH, SHIFT, STRLEN(),
TRANSLATE

SQRT

Compliance

| 2.2 | 3.0 |

Syntax

SQRT(y).

Definition

Square root of floating-point number y, for $y \geq 0$.

Cross-reference

See also Arithmetic functions

START-OF-SELECTION

Compliance

| 2.2 | 3.0 |

Syntax

`START-OF-SELECTION.`

Definition

Event triggered after the selection screen has been processed and before the LDB reader triggers the first GET event. Any code block between the REPORT statement and the first event statement is processed before the START-OF-SELECTION event is triggered.
If there is more than one START-OF-SELECTION statement, the code following each will be processed in the order in which the statements appear.

Cross-reference

See also Events, INITIALIZATION

STATICS

Compliance

3.0

Syntax

`STATICS fl.`

Definition

Declares the static variable in a subroutine (that is, FORM or FUNCTION). The syntax is identical to DATA. A static variable is a local variable that retains its value between subsequent calls to the subroutine.

Cross-reference

See also CONSTANTS, DATA, LOCAL, TABLES, TYPES

Status

See Pf-status

STOP

Compliance

| 2.2 | 3.0 |

Syntax

STOP.

Definition

Cancels all further data selection in GET blocks; no further tables are read. Jumps immediately to the END OF SELECTION event.

Cross-reference

See also CHECK, CONTINUE, EXIT, LEAVE, REJECT

String comparisons

See Operators (String Comparison)

String handling

Definition

`'Delimit strings with single-quotes.'`

Use two single quotes for an apostrophe:

`"I said "I can''t go."'` → `I said "I can't go"`.

Shifting and substrings:

`s1 = s2+c2(w2)` results in `s1` containing the substring of `s2` from zero-based offset `c2` for width `w2`.

`s1+c1(w1) = s2+c2(w2)` results in `s1` containing that substring of `s2` at offset `c1` for width `w1`.

For example:

`s1 = '1234567890'.`

`S2 = 'ABCDEFGHIJ'.`

`s1+5(3) = s2+2(1).` → `s1` contains `'12345B  90'`.

You can wrap a string across lines without closing it with a single-quote at the end of the line. Any spaces remaining on the right end of the first line or left end of the next line will be inserted into the output.

For example:

```
....:....| ....:....| ....:....| ....:....|
....:....| ....:....| ....:....|..
       WRITE: 'This is a demonstration of wrapping a
textline', / 'without breaking it in the source.',
/ 'It''s ugly but it works.'.
→
This is a demonstration of wrapping a textline
without breaking it in the source.
It's ugly but it works.
```

String processing commands

CONCATENATE, CONDENSE, OVERLAY, REPLACE, SEARCH, SHIFT, SPLIT, STRLEN(), TRANSLATE and the string-processing function modules in function group CSTR (use transaction *ISE37 [Function group [Find* to examine the available functions)

STRLEN

Compliance

Syntax

STRLEN(s1).

Definition

A system function that returns the width of s1 to the last nonspace character. The argument s1 must be separated from the parentheses by spaces.

Example

DATA w(3) TYPE I, name(36) VALUE 'Que Computer Books'.
w = STRLEN(s). → w contains 18

Cross-reference

See also the other string processing commands: CONCATENATE, CONDENSE, OVERLAY, REPLACE, SEARCH, SHIFT, SPLIT, TRANSLATE

SUBMIT

Compliance

2.2 **3.0** for the main command

3.0 for options marked with [3.0]

Syntax

```
SUBMIT rpt1

[AND RETURN

[EXPORTING LIST TO MEMORY | TO SAP-SPOOL]] [3.0]

[LINE-SIZE w1]

[LINE-COUNT n1]

[USING SELECTION SET v1]

[USING SELECTION-SETS OF PROGRAM rpt2] [3.0]

[VIA SELECTION-SCREEN]

[ WITH { p1 OP f1 [SIGN s1]

    | p1 [NOT] BETWEEN f2 AND f3 [SIGN s2]

    | p1 IN rtab}].
```

Definition

Runs report `rpt1` without returning to the calling program. AND
RETURN returns to the calling program upon completion. `v1` is a vari-
ant. `rpt1` and `rpt2` must use identical PARAMETERS and SELECT-
OPTIONS. VIA SELECTION-SCREEN re-displays the selection screen
and permits the user to edit the original entries. `OP` = EQ | NE |
GT | GE | LT | LE | CP | NP as defined in Operators (Rela-
tional). `s1` and `s2` = 'I' (include—the default) or 'E' (exclude). `rtab`
was defined with the RANGES command. LEAVE in the called report
returns immediately to the calling program.

Cross-reference

See also CALL DIALOG, CALL FUNCTION, CALL TRANSACTION

Subroutine

See FORM

SUBTRACT

Compliance

| 2.2 | 3.0 |

Syntax

SUBTRACT a FROM b.

Definition

Equivalent to b = b−a. Non-numeric fields are converted; see "Type Conversions" for conversion information.

Cross-reference

See also ADD, DIVIDE, MOVE, MULTIPLY

SUBTRACT-CORRESPONDING

Compliance

| 2.2 | 3.0 |

Syntax

```
SUBTRACT-CORRESPONDING array1 FROM array2.
```

Definition

If `array1` and `array2` are structured work areas such as header lines, then this command subtracts **like-named** fields from `array1` and `array2`. It's equivalent to:

```
SUBTRACT array1-key1 FROM array2-key1.
SUBTRACT array1-key2 FROM array2-key2.
. . .
```

Cross-reference

See also ADD-CORRESPONDING, DIVIDE-CORRESPONDING, MOVE-CORRESPONDING, MULTIPLY-CORRESPONDING

SUM

Compliance

Syntax

```
SUM.
```

Definition

Sums all the numeric (F, I, P) fields in the `itab` in a LOOP AT `itab` . . .ENDLOOP structure over the range defined by the condition block in which the SUM command is found. Places the sums in the header line of `itab` or the explicitly declared work area `wa`. Specifically, in AT FIRST and AT LAST blocks it produces grand totals of the (F, I, P) fields, and in AT END OF `f1` and AT NEW `f1` blocks it produces sub-totals of the (F, I, P) fields for all records having the current value of `f1`. For extracted datasets, use SUM().

SUM()

Compliance

2.2   3.0

Syntax

SUM(keyfield).

Definition

A system function available in LOOP structures on sorted extracted dataset where keyfield is one of the sort keys and is a numeric field. Within the processing block AT LAST...ENDAT, SUM(keyfield) returns the sum of the values of keyfield in the extract. Within the processing block AT END OF testfield...ENDAT, SUM(keyfield) returns the sum of the values of keyfield for the current value of testfield. For LOOP AT itab, see SUM.

Cross-reference

See also AT END OF, AT LAST, CNT(), EXTRACT, FIELD-GROUPS, INSERT, LOOP, SORT

SUMMARY

Compliance

2.2   3.0

Syntax

SUMMARY.

Definition

Sets the output format to the "summary" mode; use instead FORMAT
INTENSIFIED ON for clarity.

SUPPRESS DIALOG

Compliance

| 2.2 | 3.0 |

Syntax

SUPPRESS DIALOG.

Definition

In a PBO, stops showing the current screen. Dialog continues as usual,
and the next screen will be shown.

Switch command

See CASE

System

See SAPSYSTEM

System fields

For a list of the system fields SY-XXXXX see Parts II "System Fields
(Sorted by description)" and III "System Fields (Sroted by name)".

Table types

Definition

Table 1.17   Types of SAP Tables

Name	Type	Description
transparent	dbtab	Database table containing master or transaction data
pool	dbtab	Obsolete in 3.1; bulk storage of many logical tables in a database table
internal	itab	Empty structure or working data just during the current program
view	dbtab	Hierarchy of transparent tables, linking transaction data and master data
cluster	dbtab	Obsolete in 3.0; flat table with "hierarchical" appearance
structure	-	dbtab structure with no contents, such as BDCDATA; used to create itabs

TABLES

Compliance

Syntax

```
TABLES: dbtab, *dbtab.
```

Definition

Establishes a link to the named database table, view or structure (created in transaction *SE11*), and declares a header line with the same name and structure as the linked object. `*dbtab` declares a work area with the structure of `dbtab`.

Cross-reference

See also Header line, CONSTANTS, DATA, LOCAL, STATICS, TYPES, Work area

TAN

Compliance

| 3.0 |

Syntax

TAN(y).

Definition

Tangent of floating-point number y, for y in radians.

Cross-reference

See also Arithmetic functions

TANH

Compliance

| 3.0 |

Syntax

TANH(y).

Definition

Hyperbolic tangent of floating-point number y.

Cross-reference

See also Arithmetic functions

TemSe

Definition

"Temporary Sequential" file that contains the actual data for the spooler to send to the printers.

Templates

See Patterns

TEMU

Definition

(SAPTEMU) obsolete term for SAPGUI.

Text Elements

Definition

Each program has an associated pool of text elements in which you can store strings in several languages that will be presented to the user. If the user's log-in language is included in the text pool, then the strings will be presented in that language, otherwise in the development language. Maintain the text pool in transaction *ISE38 [Text elements* or from the ABAP/4 Editor *{GoTo {Text Elements*. The text pool can contain the following types of strings:

- Report or program titles
- List headings
- Column headings
- Selection texts (screen labels for PARAMETERS and SELECT-OPTIONS)
- Numbered Text (constant text passages)

Insert a numbered text element in code, screens, and so on, in either of two ways where nnn is its three-character identifier:

- TEXT-nnn
- 'descriptive string' (nnn) "where the descriptive string is inserted if nnn is empty

Cross-reference

See also DELETE TEXTPOOL, INSERT TEXTPOOL, READ TEXTPOOL

and Part II, System Fields, for the system field SY-TITLE

Time

Definition

Time is stored as a packed field containing the number of seconds since midnight (or before midnight for negative values). Time arithmetic adds and subtracts seconds, modulo 86400 (that is, midnight). See GET TIME, GET RUN TIME and Part X for the system fields SY-UZEIT, SY-TZONE, SY-DAYST .

Titlebar

See SET TITLEBAR

"Thermometer"—progress indicator

See MOVE ... PERCENTAGE

TOP-OF-PAGE

Compliance

| 2.2 | 3.0 |

Syntax

TOP-OF-PAGE [DURING LINE-SELECTION].

Definition

These events are triggered in interactive reports at the beginning of
each internally generated page break, after the standard heading is
written, and before the first data is processed. TOP-OF-PAGE is
triggered in the basic list and TOP-OF-PAGE DURING LINE-
SELECTION is triggered in lists generated interactively (detail lists).
These events are not triggered by NEW-PAGE.

Cross-reference

See also END-OF-PAGE

Transaction Codes

See Part V, Transaction codes

TRANSFER

Compliance

| 2.2 | 3.0 |

Syntax

```
TRANSFER array1 TO filename [LENGTH wl].
```

Definition

Transfers the contents of `array1` to the sequential file `filename` on the application server. If `filename` is not open, it attempts to `OPEN` it `FOR OUTPUT IN BINARY MODE`. `array1` may be a field string or a table work area. `LENGTH` returns the length of the transferred record in `wl`. A new-line character is appended to the end of record in text mode.

NOTE Trailing blanks are truncated when writing in Text mode. To create fixed-length records, use binary mode to write each record and append your own line break (CRLF -Hex 0D0A).

Cross-reference

See also `OPEN DATASET, READ DATASET, CLOSE DATASET, DELETE DATASET`

TRANSLATE

Compliance

| 2.2 | 3.0 |

Syntax

```
TRANSLATE string1
```

```
{ TO {UPPER | LOWER} CASE

| USING string2

| FROM CODE PAGE cp1

| TO CODE PAGE cp2

| FROM NUMBER FORMAT nf1

| TO NUMBER FORMAT nf2}.
```

Definition

Alters `string1` in any of several ways. `TO {UPPER | LOWER}`
`CASE` forces all characters to uppercase or lowercase. `USING`
`string2` replaces in `string1` every case-sensitive example of the first
character of each pair in `string2` with the second character in the
pair.

Example

```
DATA date1(10) VALUE '12-31-1999'.
TRANSLATE date1 USING '-/./'. → date1 contains
'12/31/1999'
```

`FROM | TO CODE PAGE` converts between SAP character codes and
those in the named code page. TYPES I, P, F, X are not converted. Use
transaction *ISPAD* to maintain the conversion tables `TCP00-TCP02`.

Example

```
TRANSLATE f1 FROM CODE PAGE '1110' TO CODE PAGE
'0100'.
```

→ Converts the contents of `string1` from the HP character set to
EBCDIC.

`FROM | TO NUMBER FORMAT nf` converts between SAP TYPE I and
F number formats and those of HP, IBM, SINEX (nf = '0000') or DEC
Alpha OSF (nf = '0101').

Cross-reference

See also the other string processing commands: `CONCATENATE`, `CON-`
`DENSE`, `OVERLAY`, `REPLACE`, `SEARCH`, `SHIFT`, `SPLIT`, `STRLEN()`

TRUE

Definition

There's no logical TYPE in ABAP. Logical state is frequently represented by a 1-character TYPE C field. with its initial value ' ' or SPACE for FALSE, and 'X' for TRUE.

TRUNC

Compliance

3.0

Syntax

TRUNC (x).

Definition

Returns truncated x, that is, the integer portion of any number x.

Cross-reference

See also Arithmetic functions

Type

Compliance

2.2   3.0 for all information, except

3.0 for information marked with [3.0]

Type

Definition

Table 1.18   The Primitive Data TYPES in ABAP/4

Type Symbol	Description	Initial Value	Default Bytes	Allowed Bytes	Value Range (Numeric fields only)
C	Text (default)	" (space)	1	[2]	
D	Date YYYYMMDD	'00000000'	8	8*	[ge] 01/01/0001
F	Float	'0.0'[4]	8[1]	8[1]*	[+/-]1E-307 to [+/-]1E+308 [3.0] or [+/-]1E-37 to [+/-]1E+37 [2.2]
I	Integer	0000	4[1]	8[1]*	$-2**31$ to $+2**31-1$
N	Numeric text	'0'	1	[2]	[2]
P	Packed	00000000	8	1-16	[3]
T	Time HHMMSS	'000000'	6	6*	-86,400 to +86,400 seconds
X	Hex	00	1	[2]	[5]
CURSOR	Table Cursor [3.0]		*	*	

NOTE   * = no width specification required

[1] = machine-specific; typical width shown

[2] = 1 to approximately 64K bytes

[3] Packed resolution = 2 x length—1, up to 14 decimal places

[4] Enclose float numbers in quotes or SAP will interpret the decimal point as a command terminator; float resolution is 15 decimal places; they may be entered in direct or scientific notation: '-1234.56', '+1.23456E3', '4', '52E-12'.

[5] Hex resolution = 2 x length

There's no logical TYPE in ABAP. Logical state is frequently represented by a 1-character TYPE C field with its initial value ' ' or SPACE for FALSE, and 'X' for TRUE.

Use packed numbers for monetary fields, and use integer fields for indexes, column numbers, positions, and so on.

If you're doing hexadecimal operations that will change the sign of any TYPE X variable, then make sure that variable is exactly four bytes wide. The sign bit may not be properly handled if the field is wider or narrower.

Example

```
DATA: x4(4) TYPE X, x6(6) TYPE X.
x4 = '00006666'.
x6 =—x4.
WRITE: / x4, x6. →  00006666    0000FFFF999A
```

(that is, the leading F is not carried forward beyond the fourth byte)

The data dictionary contains several derived data TYPES, which can be used in table domain data TYPE definitions, including:

Table 1.19   The Derived Data TYPES in ABAP/4

Derived TYPE	Primitive Equivalent	Description
AAPC	N6	Posting period in the form YYYYMM
CHAR n	Cn	Character string, n <= 255
CLNT	C3	Client (Mandt), the first key field in every client-dependent table
CUKY	C5	Set of possible currencies; referenced by CURR
CURR n,m,s	[6]	Currency field; refers to CUKY
DATS	D	Date field YYYYMMDD
DEC n,m,s	[6]	Numeric field with decimal point and perhaps sign and commas

continues

Table 1.19 Continued

Derived TYPE	Primitive Equivalent	Description
FLTP	F	Floating point field with eight bytes accuracy
INT1	1-Byte int.	Integer, 0 to 255
INT2	2-Byte int.	Integer, 0 to 65,536
INT4	I	Integer, -2**31 to +2**31-1
LCHR n [3.0]	Cn	Character string, 256 to 65,356 bytes long; must be the last field in a table and be preceded by a field of TYPE INT2 to carry its length; may not be used in a WHERE condition.
LRAW n [3.0]	Xn	Uninterpreted (that is, raw) string, 256 to 65,356 bytes long; must be the last field in a table and be preceded by a field of TYPE INT2 to carry its length; may not be used in a WHERE condition.
LANG	C1	Language
NUMC n	Nn	Numeric character field; may contain only digits, 1 to approximately 64k bytes long
PREC	X2	Sets the precision of the QUAN field
QUAN n,m,s	[6]	Contains quantities; refers to UNIT
RAW n	Xn	Uninterpreted string, n <= 255
TIMS	T	Time, HHMMSS
UNIT n	Cn	Set of possible quantity units of measure; points to table T006
VARC n	Cn	Character string, 256 to 65,356 bytes long; must be the last field in a table and be preceded by a field of TYPE INT2 to carry its length; may not be used in a WHERE condition. NOTE: This TYPE is replaced by LCHR and LRAW in Release 3.0 and above.

NOTE   [6] = P(n+2)/2) DECIMALS m [NO SIGN]

Type Conversions

SAP automatically converts field TYPES when it can. See Part VIII, "Type Conversions," for a table showing the conversions.

TYPE-POOL

Compliance

3.0

Syntax

```
TYPE-POOL t1.
```

Definition

A type-pool is a code block that contains TYPE and constant definitions you can include in your programs. You create it in transaction *ISE80* by selecting *Dictionary Objects [Edit <Type Group = 'typepoolname'.*

Example

```
TYPE-POOL t1.
TYPES: f1(8), f2(4) TYPE I, f3(8) TYPE P DECIMALS
2.
CONSTANTS: newline TYPE X VALUE '0D'.
```

Cross-reference

See also CONSTANTS, TYPE-POOLS, TYPES

TYPE-POOLS

Compliance

Syntax

```
TYPE-POOLS t1.
```

Definition

Includes in the current program the TYPES and constants of TYPE group
t1 defined in TYPE-POOL t1. TYPE groups are maintained in transaction */SE11*.

Cross-reference

See also TYPE-POOL, TYPES

TYPES

Compliance

2.2 **3.0** for the main command

3.0 for the variation marked with [3.0]

Syntax

```
TYPES u1[(w1)]

[ TYPE t1 [OCCURS n1]

| LIKE f1 [OCCURS n2]

| TYPE LINE OF itype1

| LIKE LINE OF itab1 ]
```

```
      [DECIMALS d1].
```

or

```
TYPES:   BEGIN OF u2, [3.0]
     u21...,

     ...,

     u2n...,

     END OF u2.
```

Definition

Creates user-defined data TYPES that may be used in any way the standard TYPES may be used. `w1` is the specified width of the field, applicable only to TYPES C (w <= 65535), N (w <= 65535), P (w <= 16) and X (w <= 65535). `t1` may be any standard or previously defined TYPE. `f1` may be a dbtab field or an already defined field including system fields (see Part II, System Fields) or any field you defined in a `DATA` statement. `OCCURS n` creates an `itabtype` with no header line whose structure is TYPE `t1` or matches that of `f1`. `TYPE LINE OF itype1` creates an array whose structure matches the itabtype of `itype1`. `LIKE LINE OF itab1` creates an array whose structure matches that of `itab1`. `DECIMALS d1` applies only for TYPE P. `BEGIN OF u2... END OF u2` creates an array whose elements may have any standard TYPES or any of the user-defined TYPES previously shown; elements of that array are referred to by `arrayname hyphen elementname`, for example `u2-u21`.

Cross-reference

See also CONSTANTS, DATA, LOCAL, STATICS, TABLES, TYPE-POOLS, TYPES

ULINE

Compliance

| 2.2 | 3.0 | for the main command |

3.0 for the variation marked with [3.0]

Syntax

```
ULINE [/][p1][(w1)].
```

or

```
ULINE [AT [/][p2][(w2)].[3.0]
```

Definition

Writes an underline in a report, optionally starting at position p, for width w. / starts a new line. ULINE without position and length parameters automatically starts a new line. Parameters p1 and (w1) represent position and length **literals**, measured in columns. p2 and (w2) represent position and length **literals or variables**, measured in columns. The parameters /, p and w must appear in that order with no intervening spaces.

Cross-reference

See also SKIP, WRITE

UNPACK

Compliance

 2.2 **3.0**

Syntax

```
UNPACK p1 TO c1.
```

Definition

Unpacks the packed field p1 and places the unpacked value in the character field c1. c1 is filled with leading zeros if it is longer than p1, it is left-truncated if shorter. The sign of p1 is **not** placed in c1. If p1 is not a packed TYPE, then it is converted to TYPE C following the rules described in Type Conversions. A packed field stores two digits per byte, reserving the first nibble (half-byte) for the sign, so its resolution is one less than twice its length.

UPDATE

Compliance

Syntax

```
UPDATE dbtab
[ FROM wa
| FROM TABLE itab
| SET st1 [st2...]]
 [WHERE <condition>].
```

Definition

Updates values in the database table `dbtab` from the header record. Overwrites the `dbtab` record if the key matches, and inserts the record if there's no matching key. `FROM wa` updates from the work area `wa`. `FROM TABLE itab` updates all records in `dbtab` that match those in `itab`. `SET` updates by executing the statements `st1...` of the following forms where `f1` is any TYPE field in `dbtab` and `f2` is a numeric field in `dbtab`, and where `g1` is any TYPE variable or literal and `g2` is a numeric variable or literal.

```
f1 = g1
f2 = f2 + g2
f2 = f2−g2
```

if `f2` is NULL (hex 00) then it is not changed; NULL is **not** the initial value for most TYPES.

System variables

SY-SUBRC	Description
0	Successful or itab is empty or every record in itab was updated
>0	Otherwise
SY-DBCNT	The number of fields updated

Cross-reference

See also INSERT, MODIFY

Upper case

See TRANSLATE

UPLOAD

Definition

Function module to read a local disk file into an internal table. This function module presents a dialog box to enter filename and filetype (ASCII, BIN, Excel/DAT, spreadsheet/WK1); WS_UPLOAD is similar except filename and type are parameters rather than prompts.

NOTE To insert the call in your program, use *[Pattern* [3.0] or *{Edit {Insert statement*.

Cross-reference

See also DOWNLOAD, WS_DOWNLOAD, WS_EXECUTE, WS_QUERY, WS_UPLOAD

User Exits

Definition

Extensions to the native applications may be installed at the hooks called *user exits*. The stub pools for user exits are typically INCLUDE programs with names ending in "ZZ". See on-line help *[Basis Components [ABAP/4 Development Workbench [Modifications and Improvements.*

VARY

Compliance

2.2   3.0

Syntax

```
VARY[ING] v1 FROM array1-fm NEXT array1-fn.
```

Definition

Options on DO... (VARYING) and WHILE... (VARY) that change the variable v1 in subsequent passes. On the first pass, v1 is assigned the value of element fm in the array array1; on the second pass v1 is assigned the value of element fn. For each subsequent pass, it is assigned the value of the array1 element that is further down array1 by the same separation as that between fm and fn. The elements must be compatible with and convertible to the type of the variable. If v1 is changed during the pass, the corresponding element in array1 will be assigned the new value of v1 unless the pass terminates in a dialog message. The option can assign any number of elements and the parent command can have any number of VARY | VARYING options.

Example

```
DATA:
  prodname(6),
  prodqty(2)  TYPE P,
```

```
    prodcost(6) TYPE P DECIMALS 2,
    extended(8) TYPE P DECIMALS 2,
    taxrate(4)  TYPE P DECIMALS 4,
    taxpaid(8)  TYPE P DECIMALS 2,
    BEGIN OF product,
      name1 LIKE prodname, qty1 LIKE prodqty, cost1
      LIKE prodcost,
      name2 LIKE prodname, qty2 LIKE prodqty, cost2
      LIKE prodcost,
      name3 LIKE prodname, qty3 LIKE prodqty, cost3
      LIKE prodcost,
      name4 LIKE prodname, qty4 LIKE prodqty, cost4
      LIKE prodcost,
      name0 LIKE prodname,
    END OF product,
    BEGIN OF tax,
      rate1 LIKE taxrate,
      rate2 LIKE taxrate,
      rate3 LIKE taxrate,
      rate0 LIKE taxrate,
    END OF tax.
product-name1 = 'CMR003'. product-qty1 = 3.
product-cost1 = '0.23'.
product-name2 = 'CST026'. product-qty2 = 23.
product-cost2 = '12.66'.
tax-rate1 = '0.08'. tax-rate2 = '0.0825'. tax-rate3
= '0.0915'.
CLEAR product-name0.
CLEAR tax-rate0.
DO
  VARYING prodname FROM product-name1 NEXT
  product-name2
  VARYING prodqty  FROM product-qty1  NEXT
  product-qty2
  VARYING prodcost FROM product-cost1 NEXT
  product-cost2.
  IF prodname IS INITIAL. EXIT. ENDIF.
  taxrate = 1.
```

```
SKIP.
WRITE: / 'ProdName        Cost   Qty
Extended',
            45 'Taxrate          Taxpaid'.
extended = prodcost * prodqty.
WRITE: / prodname, prodcost, prodqty, extended.
WHILE NOT taxrate IS INITIAL
    VARY taxrate FROM tax-rate1 NEXT tax-rate2.
    IF taxrate IS INITIAL. EXIT. ENDIF.
    taxpaid = extended * taxrate.
    WRITE: /43 taxrate, 53 taxpaid.
  ENDWHILE.
ENDDO.
```

results in:

ProdName	Cost	Qty	Extended	Taxrate	Taxpaid
CMR003	0.23	3	0.69		
				0.0800	0.06
				0.0825	0.06
				0.0915	0.06
ProdName	Cost	Qty	Extended	Taxrate	Taxpaid
CST026	12.66	23	291.18		
				0.0800	23.29
				0.0825	24.02
				0.0915	26.64

Verbuchen

Definition

German word for "update." Update work processes are identified as "VB" types; update components are labeled either as U1 and U2, or as V1 and V2.

Cross-reference

See also Work processes

wa

Definition

see Work area

Wait

ABAP/4 does not include a pause, sleep, or wait command.

WHERE

Compliance

2.2   3.0

Syntax

```
WHERE <condition>.
```

Definition

Qualifier that may be used in DELETE, OPEN CURSOR, SELECT, and UPDATE. The parent command processes only those records that satisfy <condition>.

Cross-reference

See also Condition

WHILE

Compliance

Syntax

```
WHILE <condition> [VARY v1 FROM array1-fm NEXT ar-
ray1-fn ...].

    ...

ENDWHILE.
```

Definition

Processes the code block repeatedly while the condition is true or until terminated by EXIT. CONTINUE unconditionally skips to the ENDWHILE for the next iteration. CHECK <condition> skips to ENDWHILE for the next iteration if the condition is false. VARY steps the variable v1 in subsequent passes; see VARY for an example.

System variables

SY-INDEX contains the one-based current step for the current nest level; after the ENDWHILE it is restored to its value before the WHILE.

Cross-reference

See also CASE, Condition, DO, IF, LOOP

Wildcards

See Patterns

WINDOW

Compliance

| 2.2 | | 3.0 | for the main command |

| 3.0 | for options marked with [3.0] |

Syntax

```
WINDOW STARTING AT c1 r1 [ENDING AT c2 r2]

[WITH FRAME [TITLE t1]] . [3.0]
```

Definition

In list processing, places a modal dialog box on the list. Subsequent WRITE statements appear in the dialog box until the end of the current event. WITH FRAME surrounds the window with a frame. TITLE t1 places the contents of t1 in the center of the top of the frame. Use Screen Painter selection *List_in_a_Dialog_Box* if using a GUI status.

Cross-reference

See also CALL SCREEN

Work area

Work processes

Definition

SAP activities set up to process user and system requests. They include:

Dialog work processes (user activities)—DIA type

Background work processes—BTC type

Update work processes—VB type (that is, "Verbuchen")

Spool work processes—SPO type

Enqueue (locking) work processes—ENQ type

Cross-reference

See also Dispatcher, Instance, Verbuchen

WRITE

Compliance

2.2 **3.0** for the main command

3.0 for the options and variations marked with [3.0]

Syntax

```
WRITE [/][p1][(w1)] f1 [attr1] [fmt1]
[AS CHECKBOX].
```

or

```
WRITE [AT [/][p2][(w2)]] f1 [attr1] [fmt1]
[AS {CHECKBOX | SYMBOL | ICON | LINE}]. [3.0]
```

Definition

Displays field f1 in a report. f1 may be a variable, a table field, a field-symbol, a literal string or a text-element. The dimensioning parameters /, p and w must appear in that order with no intervening spaces; / starts a new line. p1 and (w1) represent position and length **literals**, measured in columns. p2 and (w2) represent position and length **literals or variables**, measured in columns. Without positioning parameters, the first field starts in column one, and subsequent fields are spaced by one blank. attr1 may be one or more of the attributes shown in the following table. fmt1 may be one or more of the options described in the FORMAT command.

WRITE

Table 1.20   Attribute Options in the WRITE Command

Option	Description
CENTERED	Shows the contents centered in its defined width [3.0]
CURRENCY w1	Shown with number of decimals specified in table TCURX for currency type w1
DECIMALS d1	TYPES F I P; rounds up to d1 decimal places or pads with zeros to fill d1 decimal places
DD/MM/YY[YY]	Date field options
MM/DD/YY[YY]	Date field options
DDMMYY	Date field options
MMDDYY	Date field options
YYMMDD	Date field options
EXPONENT e1	TYPE F; sets the exponent to e1, decimal point of mantissa is adjusted to fit
LEFT-JUSTIFIED	Left-justifies the contents in its defined width (default for TYPES C D N T X) [3.0]
NO-GAP	Suppresses the space normally inserted after f1
NO-SIGN	The sign is not shown for TYPES F I P
NO-ZERO	Leading zeros and zero fields are shown as blanks
RIGHT-JUSTIFIED	Right-justifies the contents in its defined width (default for TYPES F I P) [3.0]
ROUND r1	TYPE P; moves decimal point left (r1>0) or right and shows with DECIMALS value
UNDER g1	Aligns with the starting column of field g1 in this or a previous WRITE command; g1 may be a TEXT-nnn field.
UNIT u1	TYPE P; shown with number of decimals specified in T006 for unit type u1 [3.0]
USING EDIT MASK m1	Writes the contents of f1 by using the pattern contained in the mask m1. See the following example.

- '_' (underscore) writes one character from f1

Option	Description
	• `'V'` shows the negative sign location for TYPE `P` or `I` fields (beginning or end)
	• `'LL'` at the beginning of the mask left-justifies the output
	• `'RR'` at the beginning of the mask right-justifies the output
	• All other mask characters appear literally in the output
`USING NO EDIT MASK`	Disables the conversion routine associated with the dictionary domain of `f1`

`AS CHECKBOX` places an empty checkbox on screen; the user may click on it to set the field to 'X' which is then available in `READ LINE ..` `FIELD VALUE`.

`AS SYMBOL` [3.0] places a symbol on the screen; INCLUDE either system include <SYMBOL> or <LIST> and get the names of the symbols from the include. Most symbols are one character wide; get the width of any symbol with `DESCRIBE FIELD`.

`AS ICON` [3.0] places an icon on the screen; INCLUDE either system include <ICON> or <LIST> and get the names of the symbols from the include. Most icons are two characters wide; get the width of any symbol with `DESCRIBE FIELD`.

`AS LINE` [3.0] places a line-draw character on the screen; INCLUDE either system include <LINE> or <LIST> and get the names of the characters from the include. Normally, SAP will automatically draw box corners and the like when you write lines with `'_'` or SY-ULINE and with `' | '` or SY-VLINE;for complex or dense structures, you may need to force those characters in some places.

Examples

ROUND

```
DATA: p1 TYPE P VALUE '-765.4321' DECIMALS 3.
WRITE: / p1.              →          765.432-
WRITE: / p1 ROUND 0.      →          765.432-
WRITE: / p1 ROUND 1.      →           76.543-
```

WRITE

```
WRITE: / p1 ROUND 2.        →          7.654-
WRITE: / p1 ROUND 3.        →          0.765-
WRITE: / p1 ROUND 4.        →          0.077-
WRITE: / p1 ROUND -1.       →      7,654.320-
WRITE: / p1 ROUND -2.       →     76,543.200-
WRITE: / p1 ROUND -3.       →    765,432.000-
```

USING MASK

```
DATA: c1(4) VALUE 'ABCD',
      i1 TYPE I VALUE '-1234',
      p1 TYPE P VALUE '-1234'.
WRITE: /     c1 USING EDIT MASK '__:__'.
AB:C
WRITE: /(15) c1 USING EDIT MASK '__:__'.
AB:CD
WRITE: /(15) c1 USING EDIT MASK '__:_'.
AB:C
WRITE: /(15) c1 USING EDIT MASK 'RR__:__'.
AB:CD
WRITE: /(15) c1 USING EDIT MASK 'RRR__:__'.
RAB:CD
WRITE: /(15) c1 USING EDIT MASK '_a_b_c_d'.
AaBbCcDd
WRITE: /(15) i1 USING EDIT MASK '____'.
1234
WRITE: /(15) i1 USING EDIT MASK '____V'.
1234-
WRITE: /(15) i1 USING EDIT MASK 'V____'.            -
1234
WRITE: /(15) i1 USING EDIT MASK 'RRV____'.
-1234
WRITE: /(15) p1 USING EDIT MASK '____'.
1234
WRITE: /(15) p1 USING EDIT MASK '____V'.
1234-
WRITE: /(15) p1 USING EDIT MASK 'V____'.            -
1234
```

Cross-reference

See also POSITION, PRINT-CONTROL, SKIP, ULINE

WRITE ... TO

Compliance

| 2.2 | 3.0 |

Syntax

```
WRITE f1 TO {f3 | itab}[+p1][(w1)] [fmt1] [INDEX
ndx1].
```

Definition

Overwrites character field `f3` or header line `itab`, beginning at offset `p1` for width `w1`, with the contents of `f1`, which has been formatted to specification `fmt1`. Parameters `p1` and `w1` may be literals or variables. If parameter `w1` is used, then it overwrites just that width of `f3`; if it is not used, then it overwrites the entire original value of `f3`. `INDEX ndx1` overwrites record `ndx1` of internal table `itab`.

Cross-reference

ee also `=`, `MOVE`

WS_DOWNLOAD

Compliance

| 2.2 | 3.0 |

Syntax

```
CALL FUNCTION 'WS_DOWNLOAD'

EXPORTING

  BIN_FILESIZE    = ' ' "File length for binary files
```

WS_DOWNLOAD

```
        CODEPAGE      = ' '  "'IBM' for downloading to Windows
systems

        FILENAME      = ' '  "Name of the file

        FILETYPE      = ' '  "File type (see folowing)

        MODE          = ' '  "Overwrite = ' ', Append = 'A'

        WK1_N_FORMAT  = ' '  "Format for value columns (spread
                              sheet)

        WK1_N_SIZE    = ' '  "Column width for value columns

        WK1_T_FORMAT  = ' '  "Format for text columns (spread
                              sheet)

        WK1_T_SIZE    = ' '  "Column width for text columns

    IMPORTING

        FILELENGTH    =       "Quantity of bytes transferred

    TABLES

        DATA_TAB      =       "itab containing the data to down-
                              load

    EXCEPTIONS

        FILE_OPEN_ERROR      = 01  "File cannot be opened

        FILE_WRITE_ERROR     = 02  "File cannot be written

        INVALID_FILESIZE     = 03  "Invalid parameter
                                    BIN_FILESIZE

        INVALID_TABLE_WIDTH  = 04  "Invalid table structure

        INVALID_TYPE         = 05  "Invalid value for parameter
                                    FILETYPE

        NO_BATCH             = 06  "Frontend function cannot be
executed in the background
```

Definition

Function module to store an internal table to a local disk file on the Presentation server. The calling program must provide filename and type (ASCII, BIN, Excel/DAT, spreadsheet/WK1); DOWNLOAD is similar except it prompts for file and type.

NOTE To insert the call in your program, use *[Pattern* [3.0] or *{Edit {Insert statement;.*

Table 1.21	Filetype Options
Type	**Description**
ASC	records are terminated by end-of-line characters
BIN	itab must contain at least one TYPE X field; file size must be specified in BIN_FILESIZE
DAT	Excel file format
WK1	spreadsheet format

Cross-reference

See also DOWNLOAD, UPLOAD, WS_EXECUTE, WS_QUERY, WS_UPLOAD

WS_EXECUTE

Compliance

Syntax

```
CALL FUNCTION 'WS_EXECUTE'

   EXPORTING

      COMMANDLINE   = ' '   "Parameters (command line)

      INFORM        = ' '   "Activating the confirmation from...

      PROGRAM       = ' '   "Path + name of the program

      STAT          = ' '   "Dialog parameters
```

WS_EXECUTE

```
            WINID        = ' '  "Dialog parameters

        IMPORTING

            RBUFF        =      "Dialog parameters

        EXCEPTIONS

            NO_BATCH     = 03   "Frontend function cannot be
                                 executed in the background

        PROG_NOT_FOUND = 04.  "Program couldn't be found to
                                 execute
```

Definition

Function module to launch a local program on the Presentation server.
The calling program must provide the filename.

NOTE   To insert the call in your program, use *[Pattern* [3.0] or *{Edit
{Insert statement;*.

Cross-reference

See also DOWNLOAD, UPLOAD, WS_DOWNLOAD, WS_QUERY,
WS_UPLOAD

WS_QUERY

Compliance

| 2.2 | 3.0 |

Syntax

```
CALL FUNCTION 'WS_QUERY'

    EXPORTING

        ENVIRONMENT   = ' '  "Variable name for environment
                              query

        FILENAME      = ' '  "File name for DE, FE, FL
```

QUERY	=	' '	"Query command (see following)
WINID	=	' '	"Window ID for window query WI

IMPORTING

RETURN	=		"Result of the query

EXCEPTIONS

INV_QUERY	=	01	"Incorrect value for parameter

QUERY

NO_BATCH	=	02.	"Frontend function cannot be executed in the background

Definition

Function module to check existence and attributes of a local disk file on the Presentation server. The calling program must provide the file name.

NOTE   To insert the call in your program, use *[Pattern* [3.0] or *{Edit {Insert statement;.*

Table 1.22   Query Commands

Command	Description
CD	Directory
DE	Directory Exists
EN	Environment
FE	File Exists
FL	File Length
GM	GMUX Version
OS	Operating System
WI	Window ID
WS	Window System
XP	execute Path

Cross-reference

See also DOWNLOAD, UPLOAD, WS_DOWNLOAD, WS_EXECUTE,
WS_UPLOAD

WS_UPLOAD

Compliance

| 2.2 | 3.0 |

Syntax

```
CALL FUNCTION 'WS_UPLOAD'
```

    EXPORTING

        CODEPAGE   =   ' '   "'IBM' for uploading
                                      from Windows sys-
                                      tem

        FILENAME   =   ' '   "Name of the file to
                                      upload

        FILETYPE   =   ' '   "File type (see follow-
                                      ing)

    IMPORTING

        FILELENGTH   =   "number of bytes
                                      transferred

    TABLES

        DATA_TAB   =   "itab receiving the
                                      upload

    EXCEPTIONS

        CONVERSION_ERROR =   01   "Error in the data
                                      conversion

        FILE_OPEN_ERROR   =   02   "File cannot be
                                      opened

```
FILE_READ_ERROR        =   03    "File cannot be read

INVALID_TABLE_WIDTH    =   04    "Invalid table struc-
                                 ture

INVALID_TYPE           =   05    "Incorrect parameter
                                 FILETYPE

NO_BATCH               =   06    "Frontend function
                                 cannot be executed
                                 in the background
```

Definition

Function module to read a local disk file from the Presentation server into an internal table. The calling program must provide the filename and type (ASCII, BIN, Excel/DAT, spreadsheet/WK1). UPLOAD is similar except it prompts for file and type.

NOTE To insert the call in your program, use *[Pattern* [3.0] or *{Edit {Insert statement;*.

Table 1.23   Filetype Options

Type	Description
ASC	Records are terminated by end-of-line characters
BIN	Binary format
DAT	Excel file format
WK1	Spreadsheet format

Cross-reference

See also DOWNLOAD, UPLOAD, WS_DOWNLOAD, WS_EXECUTE, WS_QUERY

York-Mills Notation

See Part XII

SYSTEM FIELDS (SORTED BY DESCRIPTION)

Table 2.1 System Fields

Field	Description	Data name	Len	Element
PREFX	ABAP/4 prefix for background jobs	CHAR	3	SYPREFX
SUBTY	ABAP/4: Call type for SUBMIT	RAW	1	SYSUBTY
BATCH	Background active 'X' or ' '	CHAR	1	SYBATCH
BATZD	Background SUBMIT: Daily	CHAR	1	SYBATZD
BATZS	Background SUBMIT: Immediately	CHAR	1	SYBATZS
BSPLD	Background SUBMIT: List output to spool	CHAR	1	SYBSPLD
BATZM	Background SUBMIT: Monthly	CHAR	1	SYBATZM
BATZO	Background SUBMIT: Once	CHAR	1	SYBATZO
BREP4	Background SUBMIT: Root name of request report	CHAR	4	SYBREP4
BATZW	Background SUBMIT: Weekly	CHAR	1	SYBATZW
BINPT	Batch input active 'X' or ' '	CHAR	1	SYBINPT
CALLD	CALL mode active 'X' or ' '	CHAR	1	SYCALLD
MANDT	Client number from SAP logon	CLNT	3	SYMANDT

continues

System Fields

Table 2.1 Continued

Field	Description	Data name	Len	Element
ABCDE	Constant: Alphabet (A,B,C,...)	CHAR	26	SYABCDE
ULINE	Constant: Underline (---------...)	CHAR	255	SYULINE
VLINE	Constant: Vertical bar (I)	CHAR	1	SYVLINE
WAERS	Currency: Company code currency from T001	CUKY	5	SYWAERS
CDATE	Currency: Date of rate from currency conversion	DATS	8	SYCDATE
CTABL	Currency: Exchange rate table from currency conversion	CHAR	4	SYCTABL
CTYPE	Currency: Exchange rate type 'M','B','G' from conversion	CHAR	1	SYCTYPE
CCURS	Currency: Rate specification/result	DEC	9	SYCCURS
CCURT	Currency: Table rate from currency conversion	DEC	9	SYCCURT
FMKEY	Current function code menu	CHAR	3	SYFMKEY
MARKY	Current line character for MARK	CHAR	1	SYMARKY
DATUM	Date: System date	DATS	8	SYDATUM
XCODE	Extended command field	CHAR	70	SYXCODE
FDAYW	Factory calendar weekday	INT1	3	SYFDAYW
DATAR	Flag: Data received	CHAR	1	SYDATAR
HOST	Host	CHAR	8	SYHOST
UCOMM	Interactive Rptg: Command field function entry	CHAR	70	SYUCOMM
MSGLI	Interactive Rptg: Contents Contents of the message line	CHAR	60	SYMSGLI
LISEL	Interactive Rptg: Contents of the selected line as a string	CHAR	255	SYLISEL

System Fields

Field	Description	Data name	Len	Element
WINSL	Interactive Rptg: Contents of the selected window line	CHAR	79	SYWINSL
CPAGE	Interactive Rptg: Current page number	INT4	10	SYCPAGE
CUCOL	Interactive Rptg: Cursor position (column) on screen	INT4	10	SYCUCOL
CUROW	Interactive Rptg: Cursor position (line) on screen	INT4	10	SYCUROW
WINCO	Interactive Rptg: Cursor position in window (column)	INT4	10	SYWINCO
WINRO	Interactive Rptg: Cursor position in window (line)	INT4	10	SYWINRO
LSIND	Interactive Rptg: Index of displayed list (0=base, 1=detail 1, and so on)	INT4	10	SYLSIND
LISTI	Interactive Rptg: Index of selected list (0=base, 1=detail 1, and so on)	INT4	10	SYLISTI
WILLI	Interactive Rptg: Number of current window line	INT4	10	SYWILLI
STACO	Interactive Rptg: Number of first displayed column	INT4	10	SYSTACO
STARO	Interactive Rptg: Number of first displayed line on this page	INT4	10	SYSTARO
LILLI	Interactive Rptg: Number of selected list line	INT4	10	SYLILLI
LSTAT	Interactive Rptg: Status information for each list level	CHAR	16	SYLSTAT
TFILL	itab: Current number of entries in internal table	INT4	10	SYTFILL
TPAGI	itab: Flag indicating roll-out of internal table to paging area	INT4	10	SYTPAGI

continues

System Fields

Table 2.1 Continued

Field	Description	Data name	Len	Element
TLENG	itab: Line width of an internal table	INT4	10	SYTLENG
TMAXL	itab: Maximum number of entries in internal table	INT4	10	SYTMAXL
TNAME	itab: Name of internal table after an access	CHAR	30	SYTNAME
TTABC	itab: Number of line last read in an internal table	INT4	10	SYTTABC
TOCCU	itab: OCCURS parameter with internal tables	INT4	10	SYTOCCU
TTABI	itab: Offset of internal table in roll area	INT4	10	SYTTABI
LANGU	Language key from SAP logon	LANG	1	SYLANGU
COLNO	List Generation: Current column in list	INT4	10	SYCOLNO
LINNO	List Generation: Current line in list	INT4	10	SYLINNO
PAGNO	List Generation: Current page in list	INT4	10	SYPAGNO
SCOLS	List Generation: Number of columns in window	INT4	10	SYSCOLS
SROWS	List Generation: Number of lines in window	INT4	10	SYSROWS
LINCT	List Generation: Page length in list lines (from REPORT)	INT4	10	SYLINCT
LINSZ	List Generation: Page width in columns (from REPORT)	INT4	10	SYLINSZ
LOCDB	Local database exists	CHAR	1	SYSTLOCDB
LOCOP	Local database operation	CHAR	1	SYSTLOCOP
FDPOS	Location of a sub-string	INT4	10	SYFDPOS
MAROW	Margin: lines from top from SET MARGIN statement	INT4	10	SYMAROW

Field	Description	Data name	Len	Element
MACOL	Margin: columns from left from SET MARGIN statement	INT4	10	SYMACOL
MSGID	Message ID	CHAR	2	SYMSGID
MSGNO	Message number	NUMC	3	SYMSGNO
MSGTY	Message type (A,E,I,S,W,X)	CHAR	1	SYMSGTY
MSGV1	Message variable	CHAR	50	SYMSGV
MSGV2	Message variable	CHAR	50	SYMSGV
MSGV3	Message variable	CHAR	50	SYMSGV
MSGV4	Message variable	CHAR	50	SYMSGV
MODNO	Number of alternative modi	CHAR	1	SYMODNO
DYNNR	Number of current screen	CHAR	4	SYDYNNR
DBCNT	Number of elements in edited dataset with DB operations	INT4	10	SYDBCNT
INDEX	Number of passes for the current DO or WHILE loop	INT4	10	SYINDEX
PAGCT	Page size of list from REPORT statement	INT4	10	SYPAGCT
PRREL	Print: Delete after printing	CHAR	1	SYPRREL
PRABT	Print: Department on cover sheet	CHAR	12	SYPRABT
PAART	Print: Format	CHAR	16	SYPAART
CALLR	Print: ID for print dialog function	CHAR	8	SYCALLR
PRDSN	Print: Name of spool dataset	CHAR	6	SYPRDSN
PLIST	Print: Name of spool request (list name)	CHAR	12	SYPLIST
PRNEW	Print: New spool request (list)	CHAR	1	SYPRNEW
PRCOP	Print: Number of copies	NUMC	3	SYPRCOP
PDEST	Print: Output device	CHAR	4	SYPDEST
PRIMM	Print: Print immediately	CHAR	1	SYPRIMM

continues

System Fields

Table 2.1 Continued

Field	Description	Data name	Len	Element
PRREC	Print: Recipient	CHAR	12	SYPRREC
RTITL	Print: Report title of program to be printed	CHAR	70	SYRTITL
PRBIG	Print: Selection cover sheet	CHAR	1	SYPRBIG
PEXPI	Print: Spool retention period	NUMC	1	SYPEXPI
PRTXT	Print: Text for cover sheet	CHAR	68	SYPRTXT
LDBPG	Program: ABAP/4 database program for SY-DBNAM	CHAR	8	SYLDBPG
DBNAM	Program: Logical database for the current program	CHAR	2	SYDBNAM
REPID	Program: Name of ABAP/4 program	CHAR	8	SYREPID
MACDB	Program: Name of file for matchcode access	CHAR	4	SYMACDB
SUBRC	Return value after specific ABAP/4 statements	INT4	10	SYSUBRC
PFKEY	Runtime: Current F key status	CHAR	8	SYPFKEY
TABIX	Runtime: Current line of an internal table	INT4	10	SYTABIX
TFDSN	Runtime: Dataset for data extracts	CHAR	8	SYTFDSN
CPROG	Runtime: Main program	CHAR	8	SYCPROG
DSNAM	Runtime: Name of dataset for spool output	CHAR	8	SYDSNAM
SPONO	Runtime: Spool number for list	NUMC	5	SYSPONO
SPONR	Runtime: Spool number from TRANSFER statement	NUMC	5	SYSPONR
TVAR0	Runtime: Text variable for ABAP/4 text elements	CHAR	20	SYTVAR
TVAR1	Runtime: Text variable for ABAP/4 text elements	CHAR	20	SYTVAR

System Fields

Field	Description	Data name	Len	Element
TVAR2	Runtime: Text variable for ABAP/4 text elements	CHAR	20	SYTVAR
TVAR3	Runtime: Text variable for ABAP/4 text elements	CHAR	20	SYTVAR
TVAR4	Runtime: Text variable for ABAP/4 text elements	CHAR	20	SYTVAR
TVAR5	Runtime: Text variable for ABAP/4 text elements	CHAR	20	SYTVAR
TVAR6	Runtime: Text variable for ABAP/4 text elements	CHAR	20	SYTVAR
TVAR7	Runtime: Text variable for ABAP/4 text elements	CHAR	20	SYTVAR
TVAR8	Runtime: Text variable for ABAP/4 text elements	CHAR	20	SYTVAR
TVAR9	Runtime: Text variable for ABAP/4 text elements	CHAR	20	SYTVAR
TITLE	Runtime: Title of report or program	CHAR	70	SYTITLE
APPLI	SAP applications	RAW	2	SYAPPLI
DYNGR	Screen group of current screen	CHAR	4	SYDYNGR
STEPL	Screen: Number of LOOP line at screen step	INT4	10	SYSTEPL
LOOPC	Screen: Number of LOOP lines at screen step loop	INT4	10	SYLOOPC
SLSET	Selection set name	CHAR	14	SYSLSET
TCODE	Session: Current transaction code	CHAR	4	SYTCODE
UNAME	Session: SAP user from SAP logon	CHAR	12	SYUNAME
WTITL	Standard page header indicator	CHAR	1	SYWTITL

continues

System Fields

Table 2.1   Continued

Field	Description	Data name	Len	Element
DBSYS	System: Database system	CHAR	10	SYDBSYS
DCSYS	System: Dialog system	CHAR	4	SYDCSYS
OPSYS	System: Operating system	CHAR	10	SYOPSYS
SAPRL	System: SAP Release	CHAR	4	SYSAPRL
SYSID	System: SAP System ID	CHAR	8	SYSYSID
TZONE	Time difference from 'Greenwich Mean Time' (UTC) in seconds	INT4	10	SYTZONE
DAYST	Time: Daylight saving time: 'X' or ' '	CHAR	1	SYDAYST
UZEIT	Time: System time	TIMS	6	SYUZEIT
WINX1	Window coordinate (column left)	INT4	10	SYWINX1
WINX2	Window coordinate (column right)	INT4	10	SYWINX2
WINY1	Window coordinate (line left)	INT4	10	SYWINY1
WINY2	Window coordinate (line right)	INT4	10	SYWINY2
WINDI	Window: Index of current window line	INT4	10	SYWINDI

SYSTEM FIELDS (SORTED BY FIELD NAME)

Field	Description	Data name	Len	Element
ABCDE	Constant: Alphabet (A,B,C,...)	CHAR	26	SYABCDE
APPLI	SAP applications	RAW	2	SYAPPLI
BATCH	Background active 'X' or ' '	CHAR	1	SYBATCH
BATZD	Background SUBMIT: Daily	CHAR	1	SYBATZD
BATZM	Background SUBMIT: Monthly	CHAR	1	SYBATZM
BATZO	Background SUBMIT: Once	CHAR	1	SYBATZO
BATZS	Background SUBMIT: Immediately	CHAR	1	SYBATZS
BATZW	Background SUBMIT: Weekly	CHAR	1	SYBATZW
BINPT	Batch input active 'X' or ' '	CHAR	1	SYBINPT
BREP4	Background SUBMIT: Root name of request report	CHAR	4	SYBREP4
BSPLD	Background SUBMIT: List output to spool	CHAR	1	SYBSPLD
CALLD	CALL mode active 'X' or ' '	CHAR	1	SYCALLD

continues

System Fields (Sorted by Field Name)

continued

Field	Description	Data name	Len	Element
CALLR	Print: ID for print dialog function	CHAR	8	SYCALLR
CCURS	Currency: Rate specification/result	DEC	9	SYCCURS
CCURT	Currency: Table rate from currency conversion	DEC	9	SYCCURT
CDATE	Currency: Date of rate from currency conversion	DATS	8	SYCDATE
COLNO	List Generation: Current column in list	INT4	10	SYCOLNO
CPAGE	Interactive Rptg: Current page number	INT4	10	SYCPAGE
CPROG	Runtime: Main program	CHAR	8	SYCPROG
CTABL	Currency: Exchange rate table from currency conversion	CHAR	4	SYCTABL
CTYPE	Currency: Exchange rate type 'M','B','G' from conversion	CHAR	1	SYCTYPE
CUCOL	Interactive Rptg: Cursor position (column) on screen	INT4	10	SYCUCOL
CUROW	Interactive Rptg: Cursor position (line) on-screen	INT4	10	SYCUROW
DATAR	Flag: Data received	CHAR	1	SYDATAR
DATUM	Date: System date	DATS	8	SYDATUM
DAYST	Time: Daylight saving time: 'X' or ' '	CHAR	1	SYDAYST
DBCNT	Number of elements in edited dataset with DB operations	INT4	10	SYDBCNT

System Fields (Sorted by Field Name)

DBNAM	Program: Logical database for the current program	CHAR	2	SYDBNAM
DBSYS	System: Database system	CHAR	10	SYDBSYS
DCSYS	System: Dialog system	CHAR	4	SYDCSYS
DSNAM	Runtime: Name of dataset for spool output	CHAR	8	SYDSNAM
DYNGR	Screen group of current screen	CHAR	4	SYDYNGR
DYNNR	Number of current screen	CHAR	4	SYDYNNR
FDAYW	Factory calendar weekday	INT1	3	SYFDAYW
FDPOS	Location of a substring	INT4	10	SYFDPOS
FMKEY	Current function code menu	CHAR	3	SYFMKEY
HOST	Host	CHAR	8	SYHOST
INDEX	Number of passes for the current DO or WHILE loop	INT4	10	SYINDEX
LANGU	Language key from SAP logon	LANG	1	SYLANGU
LDBPG	Program: ABAP/4 database program for SY-DBNAM	CHAR	8	SYLDBPG
LILLI	Interactive Rptg: Number of selected list line	INT4	10	SYLILLI
LINCT	List Generation: Page length in list lines (from REPORT)	INT4	10	SYLINCT
LINNO	List Generation: Current line in list	INT4	10	SYLINNO

continues

System Fields (Sorted by Field Name)

continued

Field	Description	Data name	Len	Element
LINSZ	List Generation: Page width in columns (from REPORT)	INT4	10	SYLINSZ
LISEL	Interactive Rptg: Contents of the selected line as a string	CHAR	255	SYLISEL
LISTI	Interactive Rptg: Index of selected list (0=base, 1=detail 1 and so on)	INT4	10	SYLISTI
LOCDB	Local database exists	CHAR	1	SYSTLOCDB
LOCOP	Local database operation	CHAR	1	SYSTLOCOP
LOOPC	Screen: Number of LOOP lines at screen step loop	INT4	10	SYLOOPC
LSIND	Interactive Rptg: Index of displayed list (0=base, 1=detail 1 and so on)	INT4	10	SYLSIND
LSTAT	Interactive Rptg: Status information for each list level	CHAR	16	SYLSTAT
MACDB	Program: Name of file for matchcode access	CHAR	4	SYMACDB
MACOL	Margin: columns from left from SET MARGIN statement	INT4	10	SYMACOL
MANDT	Client number from SAP logon	CLNT	3	SYMANDT
MARKY	Current line character for MARK	CHAR	1	SYMARKY
MAROW	Margin: lines from top from SET MARGIN statement	INT4	10	SYMAROW
MODNO	Number of alternative modi	CHAR	1	SYMODNO

System Fields (Sorted by Field Name)

MSGID	Message ID	CHAR	2	SYMSGID
MSGLI	Interactive Rptg: Contents of the message line	CHAR	60	SYMSGLI
MSGNO	Message number	NUMC	3	SYMSGNO
MSGTY	Message type (A,E,I,S,W,X)	CHAR	1	SYMSGTY
MSGV1	Message variable	CHAR	50	SYMSGV
MSGV2	Message variable	CHAR	50	SYMSGV
MSGV3	Message variable	CHAR	50	SYMSGV
MSGV4	Message variable	CHAR	50	SYMSGV
OPSYS	System: Operating system	CHAR	10	SYOPSYS
PAART	Print: Format	CHAR	16	SYPAART
PAGCT	Page size of list from REPORT statement	INT4	10	SYPAGCT
PAGNO	List Generation: Current page in list	INT4	10	SYPAGNO
PDEST	Print: Output device	CHAR	4	SYPDEST
PEXPI	Print: Spool retention period	NUMC	1	SYPEXPI
PFKEY	Runtime: Current F key status	CHAR	8	SYPFKEY
PLIST	Print: Name of spool request (list name)	CHAR	12	SYPLIST
PRABT	Print: Department on cover sheet	CHAR	12	SYPRABT
PRBIG	Print: Selection cover sheet	CHAR	1	SYPRBIG
PRCOP	Print: Number of copies	NUMC	3	SYPRCOP
PRDSN	Print: Name of spool dataset	CHAR	6	SYPRDSN

continues

System Fields (Sorted by Field Name)

continued

Field	Description	Data name	Len	Element
PREFX	ABAP/4 prefix for background jobs	CHAR	3	SYPREFX
PRIMM	Print: Print immediately	CHAR	1	SYPRIMM
PRNEW	Print: New spool request (list)	CHAR	1	SYPRNEW
PRREC	Print: Recipient	CHAR	12	SYPRREC
PRREL	Print: Delete after printing	CHAR	1	SYPRREL
PRTXT	Print: Text for cover sheet	CHAR	68	SYPRTXT
REPID	Program: Name of ABAP/4 program	CHAR	8	SYREPID
RTITL	Print: Report title of program to be printed	CHAR	70	SYRTITL
SAPRL	System: SAP Release	CHAR	4	SYSAPRL
SCOLS	List Generation: Number of columns in window	INT4	10	SYSCOLS
SLSET	Selection set name	CHAR	14	SYSLSET
SPONO	Runtime: Spool number for list	NUMC	5	SYSPONO
SPONR	Runtime: Spool number from TRANSFER statement	NUMC	5	SYSPONR
SROWS	List Generation: Number of lines in window	INT4	10	SYSROWS
STACO	Interactive Rptg: Number of first displayed column	INT4	10	SYSTACO
STARO	Interactive Rptg: Number of first displayed line on this page	INT4	10	SYSTARO
STEPL	Screen: Number of LOOP line at screen step	INT4	10	SYSTEPL

System Fields (Sorted by Field Name)

SUBRC	Return value after specific ABAP/4 statements	INT4	10	SYSUBRC
SUBTY	ABAP/4: Call type for SUBMIT	RAW	1	SYSUBTY
SYSID	System: SAP System ID	CHAR	8	SYSYSID
TABIX	Runtime: Current line of an internal table	INT4	10	SYTABIX
TCODE	Session: Current transaction code	CHAR	4	SYTCODE
TFDSN	Runtime: Dataset for data extracts	CHAR	8	SYTFDSN
TFILL	itab: Current number of entries in internal table	INT4	10	SYTFILL
TITLE	Runtime: Title of report or program	CHAR	70	SYTITLE
TLENG	itab: Line width of an internal table	INT4	10	SYTLENG
TMAXL	itab: Maximum number of entries in internal table	INT4	10	SYTMAXL
TNAME	itab: Name of internal table after an access	CHAR	30	SYTNAME
TOCCU	itab: OCCURS parameter with internal tables	INT4	10	SYTOCCU
TPAGI	itab: Flag indicating roll-out of internal table to paging area	INT4	10	SYTPAGI
TTABC	itab: Number of line last read in an internal table	INT4	10	SYTTABC
TTABI	itab: Offset of internal table in roll area	INT4	10	SYTTABI
TVAR0	Runtime: Text variable for ABAP/4 text elements	CHAR	20	SYTVAR

continues

System Fields (Sorted by Field Name)

continued

Field	Description	Data name	Len	Element
TVAR1	Runtime: Text variable for ABAP/4 text elements	CHAR	20	SYTVAR
TVAR2	Runtime: Text variable for ABAP/4 text elements	CHAR	20	SYTVAR
TVAR3	Runtime: Text variable for ABAP/4 text elements	CHAR	20	SYTVAR
TVAR4	Runtime: Text variable for ABAP/4 text elements	CHAR	20	SYTVAR
TVAR5	Runtime: Text variable for ABAP/4 text elements	CHAR	20	SYTVAR
TVAR6	Runtime: Text variable for ABAP/4 text elements	CHAR	20	SYTVAR
TVAR7	Runtime: Text variable for ABAP/4 text elements	CHAR	20	SYTVAR
TVAR8	Runtime: Text variable for ABAP/4 text elements	CHAR	20	SYTVAR
TVAR9	Runtime: Text variable for ABAP/4 text elements	CHAR	20	SYTVAR
TZONE	Time difference from 'Greenwich Mean Time' (UTC) in seconds	INT4	10	SYTZONE
UCOMM	Interactive Rptg: Command field function entry	CHAR	70	SYUCOMM
ULINE	Constant: Underline (----------...)	CHAR	255	SYULINE

System Fields (Sorted by Field Name)

UNAME	Session: SAP user from SAP logon	CHAR	12	SYUNAME
UZEIT	Time: System time	TIMS	6	SYUZEIT
VLINE	Constant: Vertical bar (I)	CHAR	1	SYVLINE
WAERS	Currency: Company code currency from T001	CUKY	5	SYWAERS
WILLI	Interactive Rptg: Number of current window line	INT4	10	SYWILLI
WINCO	Interactive Rptg: Cursor position in window (column)	INT4	10	SYWINCO
WINDI	Window: Index of current window line	INT4	10	SYWINDI
WINRO	Interactive Rptg: Cursor position in window (line)	INT4	10	SYWINRO
WINSL	Interactive Rptg: Contents of the selected window line	CHAR	79	SYWINSL
WINX1	Window coordinate (column left)	INT4	10	SYWINX1
WINX2	Window coordinate (column right)	INT4	10	SYWINX2
WINY1	Window coordinate (line left)	INT4	10	SYWINY1
WINY2	Window coordinate (line right)	INT4	10	SYWINY2
WTITL	Standard page header indicator	CHAR	1	SYWTITL
XCODE	Extended command field	CHAR	70	SYXCODE

COMMANDS AND TRANSACTION CODES (SORTED BY DESCRIPTION)

Table 4.1 Transaction codes

TCode	Description
ST22	ABAP dump analysis
SE12	ABAP/4 Dictionary display
SE11	ABAP/4 Dictionary maintenance
SE38	ABAP/4 editor
SE37	ABAP/4 Function library
SQ02	ABAP/4 Query—functional areas
SQ03	ABAP/4 Query—user groups
SQ01	ABAP/4 Query develop and execute
SE39	ABAP/4 Split-screen editor
SE30	ABAP/4 Trace
S001	ABAP/4 Workbench (CASE menu)
F040	Archive data
SU20	Authorization fields maintenance
SU21	Authorization object maintenance
SM36	Batch job definition
SM35	Batch job monitoring
SM37	Batch job overview (status)

continues

Transaction Codes

Table 4.1   Continued

TCode	Description
SB01	Business Navigator—component view
SB02	Business Navigator—process view
SE01	Correction and Transport System [2.2] (Use SE09 in [3.0])
SE15	Data Dictionary Information System
SD11	Data Modeler
SE14	Database utility
ST11	Error log files
SE35	Dialog modules
SM12	Display locks
SMX	Display own jobs
SMEN	Dynamic menu
SDBE	Explain SQL
SE73	Font maintenance
SHDG	Global values
SM59	Display and maintain RFC destinations (Install third-party products)
SE63	Language translation of field labels
SM01	Lock transactions
SA01	Locking
ALDB	Logical database manager
SE36	Logical Databases
SE91	Maintain messages
SE93	Maintain Transaction Codes
SE41	Menu Painter
SE80	Object Browser (Development Workbench)
SM64	Raise events
SA38	Report execution/launch

Transaction Codes

TCode	Description
SE84	Repository information
SE71	SAPScript—layout set request
SE53	Screen foreign language maintenance
SE51	Screen Painter
SM02	Send system messages
SPAD	Spool administrator
SP01	Spool manager
ST05	SQL trace
SM50	Overview of processes
SM51	SAP Server
SM04	Overview of Users
SM21	System log viewer
S000	System main menu
ST01	System trace
SM31	Table maintainer
SE16	Table view and maintain
SE17	Table viewer (former SE16)
SM30	Table views maintainer
SP12	TemSe (Spool data file) administration
SP11	TemSe (Spool data file) contents
SE32	Text Element maintenance
SE05	Transport information
SE07	Transport system status display
SE03	Transport system utilities
SM13	Update requests
SU56	User's authorizations display
SU53	User's most recent authorization check

continues

Transaction Codes

Table 4.1 Continued

TCode	Description
SU51	User address maintenance
SU50	User default maintenance
SU01	User Master maintenance
SU54	User menu
SU52	User parameters maintenance
SU02	User Profiles maintenance
SO10	"Word processor"
SE09	Workbench Organizer

TRANSACTION CODES (SORTED BY TRANSCODE)

Table 5.1 Transaction Codes

TCode	Description
ALDB	Logical Database manager
F040	Archive data
S000	System main menu
S001	ABAP/4 Workbench (CASE menu)
SA01	Locking
SA38	Report execution/launch
SB01	Business Navigator—component view
SB02	Business Navigator—process view
SD11	Data Modeler
SDBE	Explain SQL
SE01	Correction and Transport System [2.2] (Use SE09 in [3.0])
SE03	Transport system utilities
SE05	Transport information
SE07	Transport system status display
SE09	Workbench Organizer
SE11	ABAP/4 Dictionary maintenance
SE12	ABAP/4 Dictionary display

continues

Transaction Codes

Table 5.1   Continued

TCode	Description
SE14	Database utility
SE15	Data Dictionary Information System
SE16	Table view and maintain
SE17	Table viewer (former SE16)
SE30	ABAP/4 trace
SE32	Text Element maintenance
SE35	Dialog modules
SE36	Logical Databases
SE37	ABAP/4 Function library
SE38	ABAP/4 editor
SE39	ABAP/4 split-screen editor
SE41	Menu Painter
SE51	Screen Painter
SE53	Screen foreign language maintenance
SE63	Language translation of field labels
SE71	SAPScript - layout set request
SE73	Font maintenance
SE80	Object Browser (Development Workbench)
SE84	Repository information
SE91	Maintain messages
SE93	Maintain Transaction Codes
SHDG	Global values
SM01	Lock transactions
SM02	Send system messages
SM04	Overview of Users
SM12	Display locks
SM13	Update requests

Transaction Codes

TCode	Description
SM21	System log viewer
SM30	Table views maintainer
SM31	Table maintainer
SM35	Batch job monitoring
SM36	Batch job definition
SM37	Batch job overview (status)
SM50	Overview of Processes
SM51	SAP Server
SM59	Display and Maintain RFC Destinations (Install third-party products)
SM60	Borrow and return objects
SM64	Raise events
SMEN	Dynamic menu
SMX	Display own jobs
SO10	"Word processor"
SP01	Spool manager
SP11	TemSe (Spool data file) contents
SP12	TemSe (Spool data file) administration
SPAD	Spool administrator
SQ01	ABAP/4 Query develop and execute
SQ02	ABAP/4 Query—functional areas
SQ03	ABAP/4 Query—user groups
ST01	System trace
ST05	SQL Trace
ST11	Error Log Files
ST22	ABAP dump analysis
SU01	User Master maintenance
SU02	User Profiles maintenance

continues

Transaction Codes

Table 5.1 Continued

TCode	Description
SU20	Authorization fields maintenance
SU21	Authorization object maintenance
SU50	User default maintenance
SU51	User address maintenance
SU52	User parameters maintenance
SU53	User's most recent authorization check
SU54	User menu
SU56	User's authorizations display

SYSTEM TABLES (SORTED BY DESCRIPTION)

Table 6.1 System Tables

Table	Description
TBRGT	Authorization object and group descriptions
TSYST	Available SAP systems
TCP01	Character set—SAP
TCP05	Character set mfr
TCP00	Character sets
TCP02	Character sets—edit
TCP03	Character sets—edit
TCP07	Character sets—edit
T004T	Chart of account names
T000	Clients (in German: Mandt)
TSE05	Code templates
T001	Company codes
T005T	Country names
T005X	Country numeric and date formats
Z..	Customer-created tables that will be transported to production
Y..	Customer-created tables that will not be transported to production

continues

System Tables

Table 6.1 Continued

Table	Description
DD03L	Data dictionary tables and fields
DD02V	Data dictionary tables
TDEVC	Development classes
TDCT	Dialog module list
T015Z	Digits and numbers in text
T003	Document types
T003T	Document types, text
TFACS	Factory calendar display
TFDIR	Function modules
P9..	HR module tables
T002T	Language key, text
T100	Messages
T015M	Month names
TADIR	Object catalog
T001W	Plants
T022D	Print control for device type
TSP1D	Printer—types of formatting
TFO06	Printer barcodes
TSP0A	Printer device type
TFO03	Printer fonts
TSP06	Printer formating for device types
TSP03	Printer output device
TSP03C	Printer output device
TSP08	Printer page formats
TRCL	Program classes
TRDIR	Programs
TASYS	Recipient (target) system(s) of a transport

System Tables

Table	Description
TRESE	Reserved words
TSTCT	Transaction codes and descriptions
T006	Units of measure
USOBT	Relation transaction, authorization object [3.0]
USR03	User address data
USR02	User login data
USR04	User master authorizations
USR01	User master record at runtime
USR05	User SPA/GPA parameter values
TVDIR	Views *

(* View tables in /SE16; maintain them in /SM30 or /SM31.)

SYSTEM TABLES (SORTED BY TABLE NAME)

Table 7.1   System Tables

Table	Description
DD02V	Data dictionary tables
DD03L	Data dictionary tables and fields
DDNT	Data dictionary objects
P9..	HR module tables
T000	Clients (in German: Mandt)
T001	Company codes
T002T	Language key, text
T003	Document types
T003T	Document types, text
T004T	Chart of account names
T005T	Country names
T005X	Country numeric and date formats
T006	Units of measure
T015M	Month names
T015Z	Digits and numbers in text
T022D	Print control for device type
T100	Messages

continues

System Tables

Table 7.1 Continued

Table	Description
T001W	Plants
TADIR	Object catalog
TASYS	Recipient (target) system(s) of a transport
TBRGT	Authorization object and group descriptions
TCP00	Character sets
TCP01	Character set—SAP
TCP02	Character sets—edit
TCP03	Character sets—edit
TCP05	Character set mfr
TCP07	Character sets—edit
TDCT	Dialog module list
TDEVC	Development classes
TFACS	Factory calendar display
TFDIR	Function modules
TFO03	Printer fonts
TFO06	Printer barcodes
TRCL	Program classes
TRDIR	Programs
TRESE	Reserved words
TSE05	Code templates
TSP03	Printer output device
TSP03C	Printer output device
TSP06	Printer formatting for device types
TSP08	Printer page formats
TSP0A	Printer device type
TSP1D	Printer—types of formatting
TSTCT	Transaction codes and descriptions

System Tables

Table	Description
TSYST	Available SAP systems
TVDIR	Views *
USOBT	Relation transaction, authorization object [3.0]
USR01	User master record at runtime
USR02	User login data
USR03	User address data
USR04	User master authorizations
USR05	User SPA/GPA parameter values
Y..	Customer-created tables that will not be transported to production
Z..	Customer-created tables that will be transported to production

(* View tables in /SE16; maintain them in /SM30 or /SM31.)

TYPE CONVERSIONS

SAP automatically converts field types when it can, as described in the following table.

When making the assignment:

Target = Source

- If the target is shorter than the source, the value may be truncated and it may be flagged by or filled with asterisks;
- If the target is longer than the source, it may be filled with blanks or zeros.

The table indicates whether truncation is on the left or right end of the target, how the target is filled or flagged, and how the value is justified in the target. Codes are used in the columns of the table to show that information about each type of conversion.

Short Target (ST)—The codes used if the target is shorter than required by the source are:

- na = not applicable
- L = truncates left end of target
- L* = truncates the left end and appends a `*' at the left end
- R = truncates right end of target
- Rnd* = rounds to fit; fills with `*' when target is too short for rounded value
- OFE = overflow error

Long Target Fill (LTF)—The codes used if the target is longer than required by the source are:

- L˘ = fills left end of target with spaces
- L0 = fills left end of target with zeros
- L0F = fills left end of target with zeros or hexadecimal F
- R˘ = fills right end of target with spaces
- R0 = fills right end of target with zeros

Justification (J): The codes for justification are "L" for value is <u>L</u>eft justified or "R" for value is <u>R</u>ight justified in target.

Type Conversions

Negative Source (NS): The codes for showing how the target will receive a negative source value are

- na = not applicable
- No = no sign transferred
- L+/– = plus sign or minus sign on left end of target
- L– = minus sign on left end of target if needed
- R+/– = plus sign or minus sign on right end of target
- R– = space or minus sign on right end of target
- R˘ = space on right end of target
- 2s = Two's complement (negative hexadecimal)
- D– = negative source values are converted as 01/01/0001
- T– = number of seconds <u>before</u> midnight

In any column, → means refer to the "Conversion Details" column for more information

Target = Source	ST	LTF	J	NS	Conversion Details
C = C	L	R˘	L	na	Assigned
C = D	R	R˘	L	na	Converted to YYYYMMDD format and assigned
C = F	Rnd*	L˘	R	L+/–	Assigned in mantissa E exponent format, where 1.0 mantissa 9.99… and the exponent contains at least two digits
C = I	L*	L˘	R	R–	Assigned with trailing minus sign or blank
C = N	R	R˘	L	na	Assignment, no conversion; leading zeros remain

C = P	L*	L˘	R	R-	Unpacked; assigned with trailing minus sign or blank, and decimal-point if needed; see **unpack** for zero-filled long target
C = T	R	R˘	L	na	Converted to HHMMSS format from storage format (number of seconds since midnight) then assigned
C = X	R	R˘	L	na	Converted to hexadecimal representation (1-9,A-F) and assigned
D = C	R	L˘	R	na	First eight characters must be digits which are interpreted as YYYYMMDD
D = D	-	-	-	na	Assignment, no conversion
D = NOT D	-	-	-	na	For conversion to nines-complement date, see **convert**
D = F	→	-	-	D-	Rounded, interpreted as the number of days since 01/01/0001 and converted to date format; negative source values are converted as 01/01/0001
D = I	→	-	-	D-	Interpreted as the number of days since 01/01/0001 modulo 3,652,061 (01/01/ 10,000), and converted to date format

continues

Type Conversions

continued

Target = Source	ST	LTF	J	NS	Conversion Details
					Negative source values are converted as 01/01/0001
D = N	R	L˘	R	na	First eight characters must be digits which are interpreted as YYYYMMDD
D = P	→	-	-	D-	Unpacked and rounded, interpreted as the number of days since 01/01/0001 modulo 3,652,061 (01/01/10,000), and converted to date format; negative source values are converted as 01/01/0001
D = T	-	-	-	-	Invalid; program dump
D = X	→	-	-	D-	Interpreted as the number of days since 01/01/0001 modulo 3,652,061 (01/01/10,000), and converted to date format
F = C		R0	-	L+/–	Source must contain a floating point number in any valid representation: 3, 3.14, -3, -3.14, 3E+5, -3E5, 3.14E-5, -3.14E-5
F = D	-	R0	-		Assigned as a floating point number equal to the number of days since 01/01/0001

Type Conversions

F = F	-	R0	-	L+/–	Assigned without conversion
F = I	-	R0	-	L+/–	Assigned as a floating point number
F = N	→	R0	-	L+	Assigned as a floating point number with a positive sign
F = P	→	R0	-	L+/–	Assigned as a floating point number
F = T	-	R0	-	L+	The number of seconds since midnight are assigned as a floating point number
F = X	-	R0	-	L+/–	The highest four bytes of Source are converted from hexadecimal to decimal floating point and assigned
I = C	OFE	L`˘	R	R-	Source must contain a numeric string and may include a sign and/or a decimal point
I = D	-	L`˘	R	R`˘	Assigned as an integer equal to the number of days since 01/01/0001
I = F	OFE	L`˘	R	R-	Source is rounded and assigned
I = I	-	-	-	R-	Assigned
I = N	OFE	L`˘	R	R`˘	Assigned without leading zeros
I = P	OFE	L`˘	R	R-	Assigned
I = T	-	L`˘	R	R`˘	The number of seconds since midnight are assigned as an integer

continues

Type Conversions

continued

Target = Source	ST	LTF	J	NS	Conversion Details
I = X	-	L˘	R	R-	The highest four bytes of Source are converted from hexadecimal to decimal integer and assigned
N = C	L	L0	R	No	Digits assigned, non-digits ignored
N = D	L	R0	L	na	Converted to YYYYMMDD format and assigned
N = F	L	L0	R	No	Rounded, then assigned without sign
N = I	L	L0	R	No	Assigned without sign
N = N	L	L0	R	na	Assigned
N = P	L	L0	R	No	Assigned without sign
N = T	R	R0	L	na	Converted to HHMMSS format from storage format (number of seconds since midnight) then assigned
N = X	R	R˘	L	na	The highest four bytes of Source are converted from hexadecimal to decimal and assigned
P = C	OFE	L˘	R	R-	Packed and assigned; Source must contain a numeric string and may include a sign or a decimal point
P = D	OFE	L˘	R	R-	Converted to an integer equal to the number of days since 01/01/0001, packed and assigned

P = F	OFE	L``	R	R-	Source is rounded, packed and assigned
P = I	OFE	L``	R	R-	Packed and Assigned
P = N	OFE	L``	R	R``	Packed and assigned as a positive number
P = P	OFE	L``	R	R-	Assigned
P = T	OFE	L``	R	R``	The number of seconds since midnight are packed and assigned
P = X	OFE	L``	R	R-	The highest four bytes of Source are converted from hexadecimal to decimal, packed and assigned
T = C	R	R0	L	na	First six characters must be digits which are interpreted as HHMMSS
T = D	-	-	-	-	Invalid; program dump
T = F	na	-	-	T-	Interpreted as the number of seconds since midnight modulo 86,400
T = I	na	-	-	T-	Interpreted as the number of seconds since midnight modulo 86,400
T = N	R	R0	L	na	First six characters must be digits which are interpreted as HHMMSS
T = P	na	-	-	T-	Unpacked; interpreted as the number of seconds since midnight modulo 86,400
T = T	-	-	-	na	Transfer without conversion

continues

Type Conversions

---

continued

Target = Source	ST	LTF	J	NS	Conversion Details
T = X	na	-	-	T-	Interpreted as the number of seconds since midnight modulo 86,400
X = C	R	R0	L	na	Source must contain a hexadecimal string (0-9,A-F). Conversion ceases at the first blank
X = D	L	R0	L	na	Converted to the number of days since 01/01/0001 in hexadecimal and assigned
X = F	L	LOF	R	2s	Rounded, converted to hexadecimal, then assigned
X = I	L	LOF	R	2s	Converted to hexadecimal and assigned; only the highest four bytes are converted
X = N	L	LO	R	na	Converted to hexadecimal and assigned; only the highest four bytes are converted
X = P	L	LOF	R	2s	Unpacked, converted to hexadecimal and assigned; only the highest four bytes are converted
X = T	L	LO	R	na	The number of seconds since midnight are converted to hexadecimal and assigned
X = X	R	R0	L	na	Assigned

COMMANDS AND UTILITY PROGRAMS

Commands

Type commands in the "Command Field" in the upper-left area of every screen. In the following list, "tcode" represents any transaction code the user/developer can enter; it's always a three- or four-character string. So Ntcode means "Type 'N' followed by the transaction code."

Command	Description
/&HD	Authorizations {System {User Profile {Hold Data
/H	Debug mode
/I	Close the current session
/N	End current transaction; end debug mode
/NEND	Logoff
/Ntcode tcode	Depart current transaction and launch transaction
/O	System Session Overview
/Otcode	Create a new session and launch transaction tcode

Utility programs

Execute all ABAP/4 programs, including these SAP utilities in transaction SA38, SE37, or SE38. These programs can provide information about the R/3 system and selected programs. Simply type the program name in the entry field in the transaction and press *Enter*.

- RSANAL00: Analyses program, providing the following:

  Variable information

  Subroutine information

  Analysis messages

  Conversions

  Programs/transactions

  External tables

  Statistics

  Source code

- RSDYNL10: Lists screens (dynpros) associated with a report

- RSHOWTIM: ABAP/4 tips and tricks

- RSINCL00: Documents a program by listing its:

  Source code

  Expanded INCLUDE lines

  INCLUDE reference list

  MODULE reference list

  FORM/PERFORM reference list

  Function Module reference list

  Dialog Module reference list

  SELECT reference list

  SELECT SINGLE reference list

  READ TABLE reference list

  LOOP AT reference list

  MODIFY reference list

  DELETE reference list

MESSAGE reference list

SCREEN reference list

PF-STATUS reference list

SET/GET params reference list

Field reference list

- RSPARAM: System parameters
- SAPMSOS0: UNIX command line

2.2

EXAMPLES

Batch Data Communications (BDC)

The structure of the table BDCDATA is shown in Table 10.1.

Table 10.1   BDCDATA Structure

Fieldname	Type	Length	Description
Program	C	8	Module pool (program name)
Dynpro	N	4	Screen number
Dynbegin	C	1	'X' to Start a new screen
fnam	C	35	Name of Field to be assigned
fval	C	80[2.2] 132 [3.0]	Field value to assig

The internal table (bdctab in this example) has two types of records:

- A screen is started by entering values in the first three fields of bdctab
- Screen fields are filled, and controls are activated for that screen by entering values on just the last two fields of bdctab (the screen number is implicit until the next screen-starting record is

Batch Data Communications (BDC)

encountered). Function keys are activated by entering
`BDC_OKCODE` in `fnam` and `/n` in `fval` where `n` is the function
key number (for example, "Save" is F11 (`fval = /11`). The
records in `bdctab` specify a sequence of screen actions to
complete the transaction

The popuated `bdctab` is described in Table 10.2.

Table 10.2 Example of a Populated BDC Table

Program	Dynpro	Dynbegin	fnam	fval	(Notes)
SAPMFD02	0106	X			*first screen*
			RFD02-kunnr	rec-kunnr	*vendor #*
			RFD02-D0110	X	*"Address" box*
SAPMFD02	0110	X			*second screen*
			kna1-telf1	rec-telf1	*phone number*
			kna1-name2	name2	*test flag*
			BDC_OKCODE	UPDA	*Update (Save)*

Find the program name and screen number from *{System {Status* while
in the screen. Find the table and field name by highlighting the field
then pressing F1 or clicking on the [*?* button and selecting
[*Technical_data* from the help screen.

The transaction may follow one path interactively and a different path
in batch operation after the bdc table has been populated. If your ap-
parently valid process breaks, execute the program with displaymode
set to `A` (all) to find out if any screens appear that you didn t see interactively. You may see one or more modal dialog boxes labeled "Coding
Block" that may be blank or contain some fields. You'll need to add
those screens to your bdc table, and you may need to populate some of
the fields. The program name and screen number may be found on the
message line (typically at the bottom-left of your screen). The message
line may be obscured by the modal dialog box; move the dialog box up
to read the necessary information.

Batch Data Communications (BDC)

The following are other commands available in the bdc table.

fnam	fval	(Notes)
`fnam(n)`	`<val>`	Identifies line number `n` of the named field in a multi-line block of a form
`BDC_CURSOR`	`fnam(n)`	Moves cursor to the named screen field in line number `n` (multi-line form)
`BDC_OKCODE`	`/nn`	Press Function Key `nn`
`BDC_OKOflDE`	`/0` (zero)	Enter (This works but I've found no documentation for it)
`BDC_OKCODE`	`/8`	Continue
`BDC_OKCODE`	`/11`	Post
`BDC_OKCODE`	`CS`	F2; double-click; "Cursor-Select;" (replaces `PICK`)
`BDC_OKCODE`	`PICK`	F2; double-click; select; (replaced by `CS`)
`BDC_OKCODE`	`BACK`	F3; return to previous screen (green left arrow)
`BDC_OKCODE`	`%EX`	Depart this process (yellow up arrow)
`BDC_OKCODE`	`RW`	Cancel (i.e. Rollback Work)
`BDC_OKCODE`	`P--`	Up to top of list
`BDC_OKCODE`	`P-`	Page up
`BDC_OKCODE`	`P+`	Page down
`BDC_OKCODE`	`P++`	Down to end of list
`BDC_OKCODE`	`PRI`	Print
`BDC_OKCODE`	`tcode`	Call the named transaction

The following report program illustrates how to import data from a sequential file and use the BDC mechanism to validate and insert the data in the proper SAP tables.

```
REPORT Z_BDC_01.
TABLES: kna1
PARAMETERS:name LIKE apqi-groupid DEFAULT SY-UNAME.
```

Batch Data Communications (BDC)

```
            infile(32) DEFAULT 'bc180_abap26_exer31'
LOWER CASE,
            outfile(32) DEFAULT
'bc180_abap26_exer31a' LOWER CASE.
DATA: bdctab LIKE bdcdata OCCURS 7 WITH HEADER
LINE,
      name2 LIKE kna1-name2 VALUE 'USER01',
      BEGIN OF rec,
        kunnr LIKE kna1-kunnr,
        telf1 LIKE kna1-telf1,
      END OF rec.
INITIALIZATION.
  WRITE: SY-DATUM TO name2+11,
         SY-UZEIT TO name2+22.
START-OF-SELECTION.
  OPEN DATASET infile FOR INPUT IN TEXT MODE.
  IF SY-SUBRC NE 0. WRITE: / 'Failed to open',
infile. EXIT. ENDIF.
  DELETE DATASET outfile .
  IF SY-SUBRC NE 0. WRITE: / 'Failed to delete',
outfile. EXIT. ENDIF.
  OPEN DATASET outfile FOR APPENDING IN TEXT MODE.
  IF SY-SUBRC NE 0. WRITE: / 'Failed to open',
outfile. EXIT. ENDIF.
  CALL FUNCTION 'BDC_OPEN_GROUP'
    EXPORTING
      CLIENT = SY-MANDT
      GROUP = name
      USER  = name.    "Authorization check is on
this field
  WRITE:/ 'Opening BDC session', SY-MANDT, name,
SY-UZEIT, 'Return =', SY-SUBRC.
  DO.
    READ DATASET infile INTO rec.  "GET a record
from the file
    IF SY-SUBRC NE 0. EXIT. ENDIF.  "end of file
    SELECT SINGLE * FROM kna1 WHERE kunnr =
rec-kunnr.
    IF SY-SUBRC = 0.
      WRITE: / rec-kunnr, rec-telf1.
```

```
    PERFORM generate_bdc_data.  "load the data
into bdctab
    CALL FUNCTION 'BDC_INSERT'  "execute the
import function
      EXPORTING TCODE = 'FD02'
      TABLES DYNPROTAB = bdctab.
    WRITE:  'Return =', SY-SUBRC.
  ELSE.
    WRITE: / 'Customer not found:', rec-kunnr.
    TRANSFER rec TO outfile.  "write unknown
customer out
  ENDIF.
ENDDO.
CALL FUNCTION 'BDC_CLOSE_GROUP'.
WRITE:/ 'Closing BDC session', SY-MANDT, name,
SY-UZEIT, 'Return =', SY-SUBRC.
END-OF-SELECTION.
  CLOSE DATASET outfile.
  CLOSE DATASET infile.
FORM generate_bdc_data.
  REFRESH bdctab. "empty the table
  PERFORM generate_screen USING 'SAPMF02D'
'0106'.
  PERFORM generate_entry  USING 'RF02D-kunnr'
rec-kunnr.
  PERFORM generate_entry  USING 'RF02D-D0110' 'X'.
  PERFORM generate_screen USING 'SAPMF02D'
'0110'.
  PERFORM generate_entry  USING 'kna1-telf1'
rec-telf1.
  PERFORM generate_entry  USING 'kna1-name2'
name2.
  PERFORM generate_entry  USING 'BDC_OKCODE'
'UPDA'.
ENDFORM.
FORM generate_screen USING pname sname.
  CLEAR bdctab.  "empty the header line
  bdctab-program = pname.  "the program name
  bdctab-dynpro  = sname.  "the screen number
  bdctab-dynbegin = 'X'.  "select it
```

```
      APPEND bdctab.    "append the header to the table
ENDFORM.
FORM generate_entry USING fname fvalue.
   CLEAR bdctab.    "empty the header line
   bdctab-fnam = fname.    "entry field name
   bdctab-fval = fvalue.   "entry value
   APPEND bdctab.    "append the header to the table
ENDFORM.
* END OF REPORT
```

FIELD-SYMBOLS, ASSIGN

Use FIELD-SYMBOLS and ASSIGN to dynamically associate a value (the field-symbol) with another field. You may point a field-symbol directly at a field, or for indirect addressing, to a field which contains the name of the target field. Use field-symbols as shown in the two examples.

Example of string concatenation in Release 2.2

```
PARAMETERS: lsource(80) DEFAULT 'left string',
            rsource(80) DEFAULT 'right string',
            no_gaps DEFAULT ' '. "= space
between left & right; X = no space
DATA: p(3) TYPE I,    "runtime offset
      w(3) TYPE I,    "runtime width
      target(80).    "target string
FIELD-SYMBOLS: <fs>.
 IF no_gaps = 'X'.
  p = STRLEN( lsource ).
ELSE.
  p = STRLEN( lsource ) + 1.
ENDIF.
w = STRLEN( rsource ).
target = lsource.
ASSIGN target+p(w) TO <fs>. "points <fs> to the
substring of target
<fs> = rsource.        "assigns the right string to
the substring
```

```
WRITE: / 'Left =', lsource, ', Right =', rsource,
', Result =', target.
```

→ Left = left string , Right = right string , Result = left string right string

Indirect addressing example

```
DATA: f(5),
    fname VALUE 'Que Computer',
    lname VALUE 'Publications'.
FIELD-SYMBOLS <fs>.
ASSIGN (f) TO <fs>.
f = 'fname'.
WRITE / <fs>.
f = 'lname'.
WRITE <fs>. → Que Computer Publications
```

Logical Database Processing

This is a description of how the GET event works. The more mnemonic keyword would be GOT, rather than GET.

If you assign Logical Database ldb to your REPORT in its Attributes screen, then SAP starts an internal program when your START-OF-SELECTION event completes. That program (named SAPDBldb if the logical database is called ldb) reads every record in the logical database in hierarchical order. Every time a new table record is available, SAPDBldb looks for a GET event on that table in your program and triggers it if it exists. Every time a current table record is about to change (i.e., all the lower level linked records have been processed), SAPDBldb looks for a GET LATE event on that table in your program and triggers it if it exists. The code blocks in those events can include SELECT and any other ABAP commands. These code blocks may trigger yet other events (that is, TOP-OF-PAGE) that must be processed before the GET event can complete.

SAP delivers several Logical Databases with the system, and you can create more as you need them. They are a convenient way to report on relationally linked tables because they contain all the links, and the internal program reads all the records in the proper order. This gives you a clue about when you want to use a Logical Database. If you need to create a fairly straightforward report on the relationship defined in a

Logical Database Processing

Logical Database and if you will be writing most of the records, then a Logical Database can be useful. If your report will use few of the records, then a Logical Database is inefficient because it's going to read through all the records in the linked tables, whether you write them or not.

As an example, for the two tables linked as follows:

Table 10.3   STRUCTURE of the Example Logical Database ldb

```
header
  |
  +—subhead
      |
      +—detail
```

Example program using a Logical Database

```
*========================================
REPORT ldb_demo.
TABLES: header, detail.
SELECT-OPTIONS...
PARAMETERS:...
DATA:...
INITIALIZATION.
  ...
AT SCREEN SELECTION OUTPUT.
  ...
START OF SELECTION.
  ...
GET header. "event triggered whenever the next
header record is available

    ... "(header PROCESSING CODE BLOCK)
GET LATE header. "event triggered whenever the
current header record is about to change

    ... "(header END-OF-RECORD PROCESSING CODE BLOCK)
GET detail. "event triggered whenever the next
detail record is available
```

```
    ... "(detail PROCESSING CODE BLOCK)
END-OF-SELECTION.
    ...
TOP-OF-PAGE.
    ...
FORM...
    ...
ENDFORM.
*(eof)
```

Table 10.4   Order of Events Resulting from Program ldb_demo

Data example	Triggered events
	INITIALIZATION
	AT SELECTION-SCREEN...
	START-OF-SELECTION
header 1	GET header
subhead 1,1	
detail 1,1,1	GET detail
detail 1,1,2	GET detail
detail 1,1,3	GETdetail
subhead 1,2	
detail 1,2,1	GETdetail
detail 1,2,2	GET detail
detail 1,2,3	GET detail GET LATE header
header 2	GET header
subhead 2,1	
subhead 2,2	
detail 2,2,1	GET detail
detail 2,2,2	GET detail
detail 2,2,3	GET detail GET LATE header

continues

Table 10.4   Continued

Data example	Triggered events
header 3	GET header
subhead 3,2	GET LATE header
header 4	GET header
subhead 4,1	
detail 4,1,1	GETdetail GET LATE header
header 5	GET header
	END-OF-SELECTION

In this example, there is an intervening table (that is, subhead) that was not included in the TABLES statement; the ldb reader still marches through all its records (just to GET to the detail records), but your program has no access to them.

Pagination

Here is a brief program and its output that demonstrate some of the page-formatting features in ABAP/4. Every report contains material generated by its program plus "text elements" associated with the program and not part of its code. In the following example, the lines in the report that contain the words "text element" were not generated by the program's code.

```
REPORT PAGEDEMO LINE-COUNT 15(3) LINE-SIZE 72.

TOP-OF-PAGE.
  WRITE / 'Writing top-of-page'.
  BACK.
  WRITE 25 'Second top string'.

END-OF-PAGE.
```

```
    WRITE: 'Writing end-of-page for page', SY-PAGNO
NO-GAP.
    WRITE / 'eop line 2'.
    WRITE / 'eop line 3'.
    BACK. "to the top of the list
    WRITE 35 'BACK from the EOP block'.

START-OF-SELECTION.
  DO.
    IF SY-INDEX GT 10.
      WRITE / 'end of list; notice that End-of-Page
is not printed'.
      EXIT.
    ENDIF.
    IF SY-INDEX EQ 3. BACK. ENDIF.
    IF SY-INDEX EQ 9.
      WRITE / 'forced NEW-PAGE; notice that
End-of-Page is not printed'.
      NEW-PAGE.
    ENDIF.
    WRITE: / 'Writing line', SY-INDEX, SY-LINNO.
  ENDDO.
* END OF REPORT
```

Program PAGEDEMO generates the following report:

```
05/16/1997  Demonstration of Pagination—Text Ele-
ment Title 1
```

```
Text Element Column Header 1
Text Element Column Header 2
Text Element Column Header 3
Text Element Column Header 4
```

```
Writing top-of-page   Second top string
Writing line     3   9  BACK from the EOP block
Writing line     4  10
Writing line     5  11
Writing line     6  12
Writing end-of-page for page   1
eop line 2
eop line 3
```

Pagination

```
05/16/1997   Demonstration of Pagination—Text
Element Title 2
```

```
Text Element Column Header 1
Text Element Column Header 2
Text Element Column Header 3
Text Element Column Header 4
```

```
Writing top-of-page    Second top string
Writing line       7   9
Writing line       8   10
forced NEW-PAGE; notice that End-of-Page is not
printed
```
```
05/16/1997   Demonstration of Pagination—Text Ele-
ment Title 3
```

```
Text Element Column Header 1
Text Element Column Header 2
Text Element Column Header 3
Text Element Column Header 4
```

```
Writing top-of-page    Second top string
Writing line       9   9
Writing line       10  10
end of list; notice that End-of-Page is not printed
```

PROGRAM SHELL ZSPSHEL

Here's an example of an empty program, showing the several blocks it could contain in the order they typically appear. You may start with this shell for any new program to have consistent and convenient code blocks, and remove the blocks you don't use. This shell provides for the use of an external version control system to maintain the code.

```
*$Header: (filled in by version control system) $
************************************************************************
* (c) (copyright information here)
************************************************************************
*    Program Name: Z_____ - title
*    Description:
*    Updates Tables:
*    Input Parameters:
*    Output Parameters:
*    Return Codes:
*    Special Logic:
*    Includes:
************************************************************************
*    MODIFICATION LOG
************************************************************************
* Date          Rev #   Programmer        Description
* ----------    ------  --------------    -------------
--------------------*
*             1.0                         Original
Created
*
************************************************************************
REPORT Z_____ MESSAGE-ID ____ LINE-SIZE ____ LINE-
COUNT ____.
*
```

Program Shell ZSPSHEL

```
************************************************************************
*   TABLES
*
************************************************************************
*   SELECTION SCREEN (SELECT-OPTIONS & PARAMETERS)
*
************************************************************************
*   DATA
*
************************************************************************
*   INITIALIZATION
*
************************************************************************
*   AT SELECTION-SCREEN (all variations)
*
************************************************************************
*   AT USER-COMMAND
*
************************************************************************
*   AT LINE-SELECTION
*
************************************************************************
*   TOP-OF-PAGE
*
************************************************************************
*   TOP-OF-PAGE DURING LINE SELECTION
*
************************************************************************
*   END-OF-PAGE
*
************************************************************************
*   START-OF-SELECTION
*
************************************************************************
*   GET & GET LATE events
*
************************************************************************
*   END-OF-SELECTION
*
```

```
**********************************************************************
*    FORMS
*
**********************************************************************
*$Log:      (filled in by version control system) $
*
**********************************************************************
* End of Report: Z_____
```

YORK-MILLS NOTATION

Introduction

SAP R/3 provides a huge capability to interactive users who enter commands at the menus and screens. We found it difficult to discover and remember the sequence of commands to produce a result we wanted, so we resolved to develop a convenient and concise way to record those commands.

The following system, the "York-Mills Notation," satisfies that desire, is easy to learn and record, and can be printed in character and graphics environments. We developed it during the July 1996-1997 ABAP/4 Programming Class at SAP Canada in Toronto, whose offices are near the York-Mills subway stop on the Yonge line, hence the name.

Here's a simple example of its use, showing how to reach the ABAP/4 Editor from the R/3 Initial Screen:

/S000 {Tools {ABAP Workbench [ABAP Editor

Interpret that command sequence as follows:

/S000	→ transaction code of the initial screen
{Tools	→ press the "Tools" menu item
{ABAP Workbench	→ press the "ABAP Workbench" menu item
[ABAP Editor	→ press the "ABAP Editor" button and you're there

Purpose

The purpose of the York-Mills Notation is to record and publish the command sequences needed to accomplish work in R/3. This system is intended as an offline command record; there's no provision to automate R/3 operations. It includes the ability to package or bundle together frequently used command sequences; we call those packages macros, although they are not expanded.

Command Reference

In most programming languages, blanks, parentheses, and other punctuation marks serve as delimiters. In many programming languages, operators and various bracketing symbols are also delimiters. Table 12.1 shows ABAP/4 delimiters and what they mean.

Table 12.1   ABAP/4 Delimiters

Delimiter	Command Action
{	Menu Item
[	Button
*	RadioButton
<	Field label for data entry
\	Field label for drill-down (e.g., double-click)
/	Transcode
&	Select object (e.g., single-click)
F	Function key (1-12)
!	Shift prefix (e.g. Shift-Fnc keys)
^	Control key prefix (hot keys and Ctrl-Fnc key)
@	Alt key prefix (hot keys and Alt-fnc keys)
"	Comment to end of line
#	Macro call

Delimiter	Command Action
()	Grouping
...	Repetition, n 1 (e.g., &Field [Choose)...
..	Repetition, n 0
I	Alternative (/S000 {Tools {ABAP Workbench) I /S001
~	Optional ~&Keyfield

Command Action

Always show your starting point such as / *S000* for the main menu, or / *SE38* for the ABAP Editor.

The command action record may be shown as the name of the control or field involved (e.g. [*Enter*), or as the graphic icon for the control and must follow the delimiter with no intervening space. It should be recorded by using the same case as the on-screen string to reduce ambiguity. Separate successive commands with spaces or line breaks.

Assign a value to a label if it is required (e.g., *Maintenance Type* = 'One-Step'). The label will be shown without an assigned value if you must enter your own value (e.g., <Table Name or <Short Text).

Line Breaks

Comments are terminated by line breaks. Don't split a command action between lines. Other than those rules, line breaks are insignificant.

Macros

A macro is a list of commands, recorded with this system, that will be needed more than once and is therefore packaged under its own name. It is called in the command list where the commands it represents are needed. It is simply a shorthand way of recording frequently used command sequences.

Style Convention

The characteristics of macros are as follows:

Function	Description
Name	The macro name may be any character string without spaces and starting with a letter.
Definition	The macro definition has a header, a list of commands, and a terminator. The header and the terminator are the case-insensitive keywords "Macro" and "Endmacro." The commands are recorded by using the notation described herein.
Call	Call or invoke the macro by inserting its name in the command list where the commands it represents are needed, preceded by the macro delimiter (#).
Nesting	Macros may call other macros, but recursion is not allowed. You may nest as deeply as you wish, but deeply nested macros will be difficult for others to interpret; good practice suggests you limit nesting to no deeper than three levels.

Style Convention

It's good practice to head, foot, and comment your command list so you and others can readily know its purpose. Gather commands together in natural groups and use indentation and blank lines to make the command sequences easier to read, as shown in the following examples.

"Close a runaway SAP Session"

"SAP/R3"
"08/06/96 Dennis Barrett"
ISM04 "In another session
&the offending session
[*Close*

"Create a Simple Maintenance Dialog"

"SAP/R3"

"07/29/96 Dennis Barrett"

"demonstration of a macro although it's used only once here
Macro Choosefields (&Fieldname [Choose)... [Copy EndMacro

ISE11 "ABAP Data Dictionary

<Tablename   *"the table for which you are preparing the dialog*

[Change {Environment {Gen. maint. dialog

<Authorization Group

*Maintenance Type = 'One-Step'   *"this is for the simple dialog*

<Overview Screen = '100'

*Standard Recording routine

"Here choose the fields to include in the dialog

[Fields #Choosefields

...

"=====End of Command
List===================================

"Create a Match Code Object"

"SAP/R3"

"07/29/96 Dennis Barrett"

Macro Choosefields (&Fieldname *[Choose)... [Copy* EndMacro

ISE11 "ABAP Data Dictionary

<Object name   *"the name of the Match Code Object*

[Create <Short Text <Primary Table

[Tables

[Yes "Save before terminating Editing?

<Development Class [Save [Enter

[Choose Sec. Tab."defaults to foreign key link

(&Check Field [Choose) [Copy [Copy

Style Convention

[Fields
[Yes "Save before terminating Editing?
[Enter [Choose Fields #Choosefields
[Save [Back [Activate
"Match Code Object is now created and activated.
"=====End of Command List==================================
=======

"Attach a Match Code ID to a table"

"SAP/R3"
"07/29/96 Dennis Barrett"
ISE11 "ABAP Data Dictionary
<Object name   *"the name of the Match Code Object*
[Change [Matchcode IDs
[Yes "to Create
[Enter <Matchcode ID
[Enter <Short Text
[Choose Sec. Tab.
(&Tablename)   *"Select all the secondary tables*
[Enter
[Fields [Yes [Save [Enter
[Choose Fields #Choosefields
[Back [Yes [Activate [Back
"Match code ID is created and attached to tables
"=====End of Command List============================
===========

INDEX

STOP, 198

storing internal tables, 233-235

strings
  comparison, *see* operators
  contents, moving, 52-80
  handling, 199
  length, 200
  moving, 189-191
  processing, 200
  searching, 173-174
  splitting, 195-196
  substrings, 195

STRLEN, 200

structure
  BDCDATA table, 287
  SAP table, 206

style convention (York-Mills
  Notation), 306-308

SUBMIT, 201-202

SUBRC field, 246, 255

subroutines, *see* FORM
  calling, 48, 151
  variables, static, 197

substrings, 195

SUBTRACT, 202

SUBTRACT-CORRESPONDING, 202

SUBTY field, 241, 255

SUM, 203

SUM(), 204

SUMMARY, 204-205

SUPPRESS DIALOG, 205

switch command, *see* CASE

sy-variable, *see* system variables

synchronous calling, 167

synchronous communication, 59

SYSID field, 248, 255

system fields, 205
  sorted by description, 241-248
  sorted by name, 249-257
system, *see* SAPSYSTEM

system tables
  sorted by description, 267-269
  sorted by name, 271-273
system variables, 146, 227

T

TABIX field, 246, 255

TABLES, 206

tables
  BDC (Batch Data
    Communications), 287-292
    ASSIGN, 292-293
    commands, 289
    FIELD-SYMBOLS, 292-293
    populated, 288
    report program, 289-292
  BDCDATA
    records, 287
    structure, 287
  cursors, 140-141
  dbtab, 64
  internal, 222
    creating, 158
    editing, 77
    fields, 177
    rtab, 180
    storing, 233-235
  system
    sorted by description,
      267-269
    sorted by name, 271-273
  types, 206
TAN, 207

tangents, floating-point numbers

Complete and Return this Card
for a *FREE* Computer Book Catalog

Thank you for purchasing this book! You have purchased a
superior computer book written expressly for your needs. To
continue to provide the kind of up-to-date, pertinent coverage
you've come to expect from us, we need to hear from you.
Please take a minute to complete and return this self-addressed,
postage-paid form. In return, we'll send you a free catalog of all
our computer books on topics ranging from word processing to
programming and the internet.

Mr. ☐   Mrs. ☐   Ms. ☐   Dr. ☐

Name (first) ☐☐☐☐☐☐☐☐☐ (M.I.) ☐ (last) ☐☐☐☐☐☐☐☐☐☐☐☐

Address ☐☐☐☐☐☐☐☐☐☐☐☐☐☐☐☐☐☐☐☐☐☐☐☐☐☐☐☐

City ☐☐☐☐☐☐☐☐☐☐☐ State ☐☐ Zip ☐☐☐☐☐ ☐☐☐☐

Phone ☐☐☐ ☐☐☐ ☐☐☐☐ Fax ☐☐☐ ☐☐☐ ☐☐☐☐

Company Name ☐☐☐☐☐☐☐☐☐☐☐☐☐☐☐☐☐☐☐☐☐☐☐

E-mail address ☐☐☐☐☐☐☐☐☐☐☐☐☐☐☐☐☐☐☐☐☐☐☐☐☐☐☐☐☐☐☐☐☐

1. Please check at least (3) influencing factors for purchasing this book.

Front or back cover information on book .... ☐
Special approach to the content .... ☐
Completeness of content .... ☐
Author's reputation .... ☐
Publisher's reputation .... ☐
Book cover design or layout .... ☐
Index or table of contents of book .... ☐
Price of book .... ☐
Special effects, graphics, illustrations .... ☐
Other (Please specify): _____ ☐

2. How did you first learn about this book?

Internet Site .... ☐
Saw in Macmillan Computer
   Publishing catalog .... ☐
Recommended by store personnel .... ☐
Saw the book on bookshelf at store .... ☐
Recommended by a friend .... ☐
Received advertisement in the mail .... ☐
Saw an advertisement in: _____ ☐
Read book review in: _____ ☐
Other (Please specify): _____ ☐

3. How many computer books have you purchased in the last six months?

This book only .... ☐   3 to 5 books .... ☐
2 books .... ☐   More than 5 .... ☐

4. Where did you purchase this book?

Bookstore .... ☐
Computer Store .... ☐
Consumer Electronics Store .... ☐
Department Store .... ☐
Office Club .... ☐
Warehouse Club .... ☐
Mail Order .... ☐
Direct from Publisher .... ☐
Internet site .... ☐
Other (Please specify): _____ ☐

5. How long have you been using a computer?

Less than 6 months .. ☐   6 months to a year ..... ☐
1 to 3 years .... ☐   More than 3 years ...... ☐

6. What is your level of experience with personal computers and with the subject of this book?

	With PC's	With subject of book
New	☐	☐
Casual	☐	☐
Accomplished	☐	☐
Expert	☐	☐

Source Code — ISBN:0-7897-1416-7

7. Which of the following best describes your job title?

Administrative Assistant .... ☐
Coordinator .... ☐
Manager/Supervisor .... ☐
Director .... ☐
Vice President .... ☐
President/CEO/COO .... ☐
Lawyer/Doctor/Medical Professional .... ☐
Teacher/Educator/Trainer .... ☐
Engineer/Technician .... ☐
Consultant .... ☐
Not employed/Student/Retired .... ☐
Other (Please specify): .... ☐

8. Which of the following best describes the area of the company your job title falls under?

Accounting .... ☐
Engineering .... ☐
Manufacturing .... ☐
Marketing .... ☐
Operations .... ☐
Sales .... ☐
Other (Please specify): .... ☐

9. What is your age?

Under 20 .... ☐
21-29 .... ☐
30-39 .... ☐
40-49 .... ☐
50-59 .... ☐
60-over .... ☐

10. Are you:

Male .... ☐
Female .... ☐

11. Which computer publications do you read regularly? (Please list)

_____
_____
_____
_____
_____
_____
_____
_____
_____

Comments: _____
_____
_____

Fold here and scotch-tape to m

Check out Que® Books on the World Wide Web
http://www.mcp.com/que

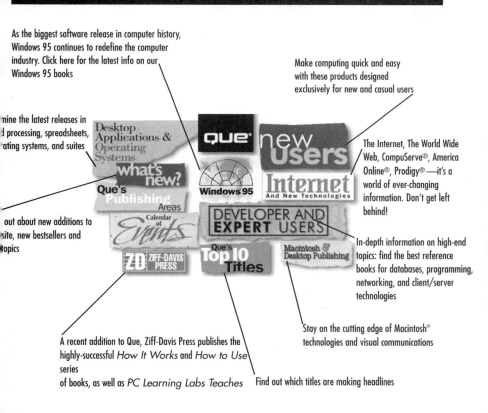

As the biggest software release in computer history, Windows 95 continues to redefine the computer industry. Click here for the latest info on our Windows 95 books

Make computing quick and easy with these products designed exclusively for new and casual users

nine the latest releases in processing, spreadsheets, ating systems, and suites

The Internet, The World Wide Web, CompuServe®, America Online®, Prodigy® —it's a world of ever-changing information. Don't get left behind!

out about new additions to site, new bestsellers and topics

In-depth information on high-end topics: find the best reference books for databases, programming, networking, and client/server technologies

Stay on the cutting edge of Macintosh® technologies and visual communications

A recent addition to Que, Ziff-Davis Press publishes the highly-successful *How It Works* and *How to Use* series of books, as well as *PC Learning Labs Teaches*

Find out which titles are making headlines

1 6 separate publishing groups, Que develops products for many specific market segments and areas of mputer technology. Explore our Web Site and you'll find information on best-selling titles, newly published titles, upcoming products, authors, and much more.

- Stay informed on the latest industry trends and products available

- Visit our online bookstore for the latest information and editions

- Download software from Que's library of the best shareware and freeware

MACMILLAN COMPUTER PUBLISHING USA
A VIACOM COMPANY

Technical Support:

If you need assistance with the information in this book or with a CD/Disk accompanying the book, please access the Knowledge Base on our Web site at **http://www.superlibrary.com/general/support**. Our most Frequently Asked Questions are answered there. If you do not find the answer to your questions on our Web site, you may contact Macmillan Technical Support **(317) 581-3833** or e-mail us at **support@mcp.com**.